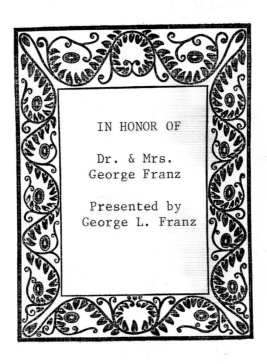

IN HONOR OF

Dr. & Mrs.
George Franz

Presented by
George L. Franz

YESTERDAY, TODAY, AND WHAT NEXT?

REFLECTIONS ON HISTORY AND HOPE

YESTERDAY, TODAY, AND WHAT NEXT?

ROLAND H. *Herbert* BAINTON

AUGSBURG Publishing House • Minneapolis

YESTERDAY, TODAY, AND WHAT NEXT?

To Elisabeth and Felix Hirsch

Contents

Introduction

Having devoted my life to the study of history, I am prompted in my latter days to ask whether one can make sense of it all. This is a personal concern. We are told that one should not approach history with a personal concern. History is interesting as history. So it is, and some subjects invite interest with no personal concern. The question of life on Mars intrigues me, though I have no thought of colonization. A book on colonial tools is fascinating, though I have no inclination to construct replicas. I am interested in totem poles but I would not think of carving a huge log with electric tools into a replica to serve as a tourist attraction in a restaurant.

History is indeed alluring for its own sake, but also pertinent to our situation for the light it may throw on the nature of man. (I use this word rather than humankind, for the term is clumsy and style is not to be despised.) If in a measure we can understand man, we may be able to foresee how men are likely to respond to new crises. Previous experience may disclose how best to insure survival, equalize opportunity, conserve freedom, achieve international cooperation and world peace. And should we discover that some ends cannot be achieved because precluded by others, or even that the race itself faces extinction, we may be braced by the examples of those who before us lived under the expectation of impending doom. The examination of human behavior will carry us soon beyond the human to inquire about God, providence, Christ, and Christian ideals. The answers lie beyond the demonstrable. Still the demonstrable may yield clues to the undemonstrable.

The Solidarity
of Human Nature

The understanding of man is according to some quite impossible because there is no solidarity of human nature. We are able to study not man but only men. Each individual is unique. Each culture is unique. Generalizations are fictitious and history as a whole cannot be fitted into any rational frame. The best we can do is to write biographies of individuals and surveys of periods. This attitude was prevalent in the nineteenth century where in Germany it was called *Historismus*. It did produce great biographies and analyses of periods. In biography one thinks of Dilthey's *Schleiermacher* and Carlyle's *Heroes and Hero Worship*. His sketch of Luther bristles with a vitality beyond many a learned tome.

But although, to be sure, every mosquito differs from every other and every butterfly from all other butterflies, nevertheless one can tell a mosquito from a butterfly. Aware of this, Dilthey went beyond individual persons to types marked by individuality that coincided with cultures in diverse lands and times. On this basis Ranke could write a work on the Reformation and Burckhardt on the Renaissance. Such achievements fill us with admiration and gratitude, but still leave us desirous of weaving a tapestry rather than assembling threads.

Failure to go beyond the individual spells more than the frustration of curiosity. Sheer individualism has tended to shatter a universal morality. For if the concept of man is to be split into millions of men, each unique, or even into thousands of types each different, what then becomes of a universal morality? There can be no values, no principles, no rules which apply to every-one. So spoke the Sophists of ancient Greece who were aware of the diversity of laws and customs. Their conclusion was that the law of nature is simply the law of power and that might makes right. To this Socrates replied that it were better to suffer injustice than to inflict it, and the concept emerged of an ethical law of nature valid for all peoples.

Ernst Troeltsch, impressed by diversity but recoiling from the utter relativism of *Historismus,* posited at first as universal values only tolerance and love for those with different codes. He was shocked into further recoil when he perceived that the difference between Germany and the West hinged on this very point. The West retained the tradition of natural law. "We hold these truths to be self-evident." Germany, claiming the right to make her own code, succumbed to Prussian militarism and was on the way to National Socialism. Let her not trample, said he, on the rights of man.[1]

Others challenge the theory of unity by noting differences, be they biological, geographical or chronological. The biological distinction has been agitated in the United States. The view has long been regnant and is not yet extinct that the blacks are intellectually inferior to the whites. Some years ago on a lecture tour I was entertained by a hostess in Alabama. A black came to cut her lawn with a hand mower. I asked whether she preferred this type to the motor. "Oh," said she, "a black would not be able

12

to operate a power mower." I hope she has lived to see the blacks driving huge trucks and functioning in roles calling for high competence. Friends in medicine tell me that blacks usually take longer to obtain degrees, since deficient in early training. Some attain the top level of proficiency and few are dropped for incapacity.

On the score of geography, Jaspers made the observation that between the years 500 to 200 B.C. a great efflorescence of culture occurred coincidentally in China, India, Egypt, Mesopotamia, Palestine, and Greece. No geographical demarcation.[2] A combination perhaps of biology and geography is to be found in the assertion that Catholicism is the religion of southern peoples, Protestantism of northern. In South America a Protestant is stigmatized as not Spanish. In reply one may note that not all of Germany became Protestant and that one of the greatest Protestant leaders, John Calvin, was a Frenchman, a Latin.

The question so interested me that lecturing in Buenos Aires in 1960 [3] I maintained the thesis that within these groups individuals so differed from each other that one could not classify them as Latin and Teuton and parallels to the individuals in one culture could better be found in the other. By way of illustration I took four Spaniards of the sixteenth century, who differed widely from each other and could better be paired with examples in England, France, Germany or Italy and even Poland.

The first was Michael Servetus, burned in effigy by the Catholics and in actuality by the Protestants because of his denial of the doctrine of the Trinity as formulated in the creed of Nicaea. He was also the discoverer of the pulmonary circulation of the blood. His theological system was a bizarre blending of biblical exegesis, Neoplatonic mysticism, esoteric lore, and apocalypticism. One cannot find anywhere an exact parallel. The greatest similarities are to be found not with any Spaniard, but with the like of Paracelsus in Switzerland, Postel in France, and the Antitrinitarians in Italy and Poland.

The second was Cardinal Ximenes, Primate of Spain, regent of the state for a time, humanist scholar, who brought out the *Complutensian Polyglot* of the entire Bible in the original tongues, a rigorous reformer of the church and the monasteries, grand Inquisitor and fomentor of a crusade. He can certainly not be matched in his own land and scarcely anywhere, but one would come close to a replica by combining Cardinal Woolsey and Thomas More, both Englishmen. Ignatius Loyola and John Calvin have frequently been compared. Both had gone through conversion experiences, both were rigorously disciplined. Both organized and directed great movements. Juan Valdes was a Spaniard operating in Italy, Spanish indeed in his indebtedness to the Alumbrados, but European in the similarity of his spiritualization of religion to Erasmus of Holland, and in Germany with Denck, Schwenckfeld, and Sebastian Franck. One can, then, scarcely say that by nature there was a distinctively Spanish type.

At the same time individuals operate within cultural frameworks fashioned by centuries of circumstances. Take again Spain. Here Christianity had long been marked by an intense orthodoxy, a close affiliation of church and state and a large independence of the papacy. The Visigoths, who occupied Spain, had, on conversion to Christianity, first been Arian heretics at odds with the papacy. Embracing orthodoxy they became strident in repudiating their theological past but did not in consequence draw closer to the pope. The later conflicts with the Moors and Jews intensified zeal for dogmatic rectitude. The subservience of the chaplain to the king carried over from the Visigothic pattern so that in the sixteenth century the word was, "There is no pope in Spain." The system was Caesaro-papism.

In the period of the Renaissance the Hispanic peninsula was

struggling to achieve a political and religious consolidation. The first was achieved by the union of Aragon and Castille through the marriage of Ferdinand and Isabella. As for religion, there was the option of alignment either with Islam across the straits or with Christendom over the Pyrenees. The choice was for the latter. What then should be done with the Jews and the Muslims? The former in 1492 were given the choice of emigration or conversion and later the Moors were accorded the same treatment. The converts, called *conversos*, were then placed under the closest surveillance to keep them from continuing to observe the rites of their former faiths. The Spanish Inquisition rooted out deviants.

Servetus as an individual operated within the framework of this culture. The question he put to himself was why the Jews and Moors should so stoutly resist religious assimilation. What impeded willing adherence to Christianity? His answer was the doctrine of the Trinity. Since it was not formulated in the New Testament in terms of the creed of Nicaea he concluded it could be eliminated.[4] Unity could be achieved by excision. His own formulation was thus prompted by a local situation. This is not to say that Antitrinitarianism could not have arisen otherwise in another form and place. In Italy and Poland it did.

Again the same individual may act quite differently in different contexts. Historical animosities may turn a kindly peasant into a butcher. Toynbee relates that when as a youth he was tramping in Greece a native gave him a ride. They looked down on a deserted village. "Where are the people?" asked Toynbee. "They were Muslims. We slit their throats."[5]

We may conclude then that human nature has not fundamentally varied by continents, by countries, and by race. But what of the centuries? If throughout the course of the years the nature of man has not been constant, prognostications are precarious if not impossible. The question of the nature of nature and its immutability has occupied all of the philosophies of history. A brief survey of the main types is in order with this point particularly in mind.

Fate and Fortune

Any system which holds that history is controlled by some force beyond man, be it the order of nature or the will of God, need not be concerned with human nature. "There is a destiny which shapes our ends rough hew them as we may." We can hew but to no avail. The outcome in the Christian doctrine of predestination is settled by God as to what lies beyond history and in classical thought within history through the goddess Fortuna construed either as fate or as caprice, combining the Greek *Moira* and *Tyche*.

As ineluctable destiny, Fortuna presided over the lives of men and empires. This was the rationale of the Delphic oracle. As examples of individuals we may take Aeschylus and Nero. The great dramatist was told to beware of a black eagle. In so far as possible he stayed in the open to view the sky but a black eagle with a tortoise clutched in its talons went to a considerable height to drop it and break the shell. It fell on the head of Aeschylus.[6] Nero inquired his fate of the oracle and was told to beware of seventy-three. He was thirty and thought he had long to sip the nectar of life; while in Spain troops were being drilled for his overthrow by Galba who was seventy-three.[7] Croesus handsomely endowed the oracle in the hope of an encouraging answer to his query whether he should attack the Persians. He was told that if he did an empire would fall.[8] He attacked. An empire fell—his own. Belief inclines some to caution, some to recklessness on the ground that one cannot die until one's number comes.

Fortuna as fate played an extensive role in the literature of the Middle Ages.[9] In the Renaissance fatalism returned with the revival of astrology, as it has again in our day. It regards human nature not as variable but as varied in accord with the signs of the zodiac. Machiavelli wrestled with the theme hoping that Fortuna might be overcome by *virtu,* human will, and energy. Fate, he saw, cannot be prevented, but may be circumvented. He wrote, "Fortune is like a raging torrent which sweeps before it trees, and houses and none can withstand it. Very true, but when it is not raging one can construct dykes and canals to contain and divert it. Similarly man's free will is not defunct and can take measure to restrain Fortune." [10]

But now Fortuna has also the other meaning, not fate, but fortune, chance, contingency, the fortuitous, the unrelated to what else is going on. Spengler cites a number of instances of the intrusion of one sequence upon another with no apparent connection but with incalculable impact; the sudden and unexpected deaths for example of Alexander and Gustavus Adolphus. Luther, he remarks, might easily have been a martyr or a pope. His ideals were not so different from those of Pope Hadrian VI. The unpredictable saved him.[11]

Spengler at that point was quite right. On a number of occasions Luther was saved by what you might call a fluke. One was when Cajetan, after an interview, told him to leave and never return unless he would recant. Luther took this to mean the end, when out of the blue came word to return to Wittenberg. The reason for the unexpected turn was news of the impending death of the emperor. The office was elective. The pope did not wish the dignity to go to a strong monarch like Henry of England, Charles of Spain, or Francis of France. The pope's preference was for none other than Luther's own prince, Frederick the Wise, and for that reason the pressure was relaxed.

On another occasion after Luther had made his speech at Worms all six of the electors were reported to be ready to put him under the ban. All six would include Frederick. But the next day, when the vote came, he refused to condemn. Luther was saved because overnight Frederick had changed his mind.[12] On another occasion, the deliverance was due to the failure of a message to arrive on time. The Diet of Worms was meeting. The church could only excommunicate. The state enacted and executed the penalty of death. A bull of excommunication against Luther required ratification by the secular diet. The pope sent a bull naming besides Luther others, including Hutten who was in a position to march on Worms with troops. The bull was returned with the request for another, naming only Luther. The new bull was so long in coming and the Diet so unwilling to act without it, that Luther was given a hearing.[13]

The reverse effect of non-communication came to my personal attention in the case of a Jewish Italian who, when Mussolini lined up with Hitler, had to go abroad leaving behind his gentile wife and a baby daughter. When America entered the war communication was cut off. On the resumption of relations he returned to discover that his wife was married to his best friend. There was no recrimination and the three formed a triad of affection.

Further examples are not lacking in our own day. The life of Toynbee was saved by a mistake on a map.[14] He was in Greece at the time. The map indicated a highway at a given point. It was not there. He took to the woods, came to a stream, and drank heavily. The water was polluted, giving him dysentery from which he did not recover for six years and in consequence in August 1914 was disqualified for military service in a war in which half of his academic contemporaries fell. "Was it providence?" he asks. "If so, what of those who were not spared?"

My own experience can add another example. At college I returned from a cross-country run after dark. The gymnasium was open but unlighted. I wanted a dip, went out to the end of the diving board and was about to plunge when I bethought me to check. I climbed down the ladder. The pool was empty. On the other hand a brilliant young professor at Yale took his three-year-old daughter for a spin in her cart on a frozen pond. He did not reflect that at the upper end a spring entered with warmer water. The child slid from the cart. He dove after her. Both died of cardiac failure by reason of the cold. Why were they taken and I spared?

From private cases one may turn again to the public. The pacific king of Greece, Alexander, was killed by the bite of a monkey and was succeeded by the belligerent Constantine, who plunged Greece into a war with Turkey. Churchill remarked that the bite of a monkey was responsible for a quarter of a million deaths.[15]

The Cyclical Theory of History

Another deterministic theory of history allows greater scope for men and consequently raises deeper questions as to his nature. This is the theory of cycles, prevalent in classical antiquity and recurrently surfacing. The cosmos is assumed to be a closed entity within which circuits or cycles revolve without ever exceeding the bounds. This is obvious in the case of the revolutions of the heavenly bodies. The moon waxes and wanes. The tides ebb and flow. The planets revolve in their orbits. Another example is that of the seasons. Every barren winter turns to verdant spring. Every blossoming summer is followed by seer autumn. Then again winter. The examples when used as analogies for human history falter because in each case it is the same moon, the same planet, the same earth which repeats its course. More precise is comparison with the life of man through the stages of childhood, youth, maturity, senescence and death. In this case the continuum requires that another step into the role. And so, of course, it is with empires.

The main point is that the scheme of cycles is deterministic and since the entire structure of the universe is set in an ineluctable frame there can be no creativity, nothing new. This conviction found its classic expression in the words of a Hellenistic Jew in the opening chapter of the book of Ecclesiastes in the Old Testament. He wrote:

> What does a man gain by all the toil
>   at which he toils under the sun?
> A generation goes and a generation comes,
>   but the earth remains forever.
> The sun rises and the sun goes down,
>   and hastens to the place where it rises.
> The wind blows to the south,
>   and goes round to the north;
> round and round goes the wind,
>   and on its circuits the wind returns.
> All streams run to the sea,
>   but the sea is not full;
> to the place where the streams flow,
>   there they flow again.
>
> . . . .
>
> What has been is what will be,
>   and what has been done is what will be done;
> And there is nothing new under the sun.
> Is there a thing of which it is said,
>   "See, this is new"?
> It has been already, in the ages before us.

The closest parallel on the classical side is the reflection of Marcus Aurelius that one need live only to be forty to know all that ever was and is to be.[16] The most graphic example of this conviction is the case of Scipio Aemilianus, who, when he had conquered Carthage, wept, not because he was selling fifty thousand into slavery, but because he foresaw the day when a like fate would befall Rome.[17]

22

The Cyclical Theory of History

There are abundant instances of this theory in classical literature. Though rejected by the Christians it has entered new cycles of its own. Witness Vico in the seventeenth century with his *corsi* and *ricorsi*.[18] He did believe in God, but excluded his intervention in history. Spengler implies inevitability as he points to the signs which presage demise. Toynbee's *Study of History* suggests a like view. Empires, he says, arise in response to a challenge, but to a subsequent challenge fail to respond. Why the failure? Not by reason of conquest from without, but of sin from within. Toynbee believes in original sin, ingrained in the nature of man. Is not the sequel then inevitable?

The explanation of the phenomenon of decline seldom in antiquity went beyond the view of the closed cosmos, but a psychological explanation was offered by Sallust. He recalled the plea of Scipio that Rome should not destroy Carthage because a state requires a rival to hold it together. Remove the outward threat and civil dissension disrupts. Sallust saw in the civil wars of his time the result of failing to heed the counsel.[19] Horace discovered rather a genetic corruption. When Romulus murdered Remus, a virus of corruption was injected into the Roman blood stream.[20] This is like the dictum, "In Adam's fall fell we all." In England of the late sixteenth century the cycle of war is laid squarely on the shoulders of man. Thomas Fenne wrote:

> Warre bringeth ruine, ruine bringeth povertie, povertie procureth peace, and peace in time increaseth riches, riches causeth statelinesse, statelinesse increaseth envie, envie in the end procureth deadly mallice, mortall mallice proclaimeth open warre and battaile; and from warre againe as before is rehearsed.[21]

The theory of cycles does have a certain validity with respect to the recurrence of patterns, Any philosophy, religion, or ethos which has profoundly influenced a generation and has then been dropped will eventually revive. This is an aspect of the conflict of the generations. The son, in rebelling against the father, reverts to some spiritual ancestor, though a millenium intervene.

Examples abound. Gnosticism, rejected by the early church, reemerged in the Renaissance in the Cabala and Hermeticism and in our own day has appealed to Jung and to a degree Tillich. The political theory of the Sophists came again to life in Machiavelli and Nietzsche. The skepticism of Sextus Empiricus revived in a measure in the Renaissance and more especially in the Enlightenment. The dualism of Zoroaster and the Manichees, which for a time intrigued Augustine, proves congenial to Toynbee.

In the arts, the classical style in the architecture of antiquity was displaced by the romanesque. This in turn by the gothic, and the gothic by the renaissance. In the eighteenth century, Gibbon derided the gothic but in the nineteenth there was a revival. In music, a friend calls my attention to the neglect of sixteenth century compositions during the next three centuries, followed by a revival in our own. In the history of the church, periods of sect formation oscillate with periods of reunion. Moral permissiveness and laxity arise in reaction to the rigors of Puritanism and then disillusionment over moral anarchy revives severe discipline.

The oscillating fashions may be due to the itch for novelty but also to the human incapacity to encompass the whole at a given time. Man like a juggler tries to keep six balls in the air. Always one is dropping. As it is retrieved another falls, eventually to be restored when the successor slips. Thus we have the ages of faith, reason, science, secularism, fanaticism, materialism and the like. The metaphor limps, however, because the fallen balls are not dormant, but continually challenge those ascendent in a jostling, swirling, pulsing whole.

The conclusion to be drawn as to the nature of man is the very obvious one of finitude. There are limits to human capacity. One would not have thought necessary to labor the point were it not for the exuberant rhapsodies of those so drunk with confidence in the unlimited capacity of man as to envisage colonizing the planets and no doubt running a daily shuttle with lettuce and oranges from California and Florida to the Man in the Moon.

But if some of the ideas of progress are too exuberant there are concepts of man and his future less lugubrious than those of the deterministic type.

Progress

The theory of cycles, prevalent in antiquity, was superseded in the eighteenth and nineteenth centuries by the idea of progress.[22]. There was an adumbration in the cyclical theory itself, seeing that one turn of Fortune's wheel was an ascent, even though ultimately reversed. There was a slight intimation of continuous advance in Virgil's prediction that Augustus would extend Rome's civilizing sway over the earth and Augustine envisaged the possibility that if emperors were Christian, empires need not be robbery on a large scale. But the concept came of age only in the period of revolutions and enlightenment and reached the crest with the staggering advance in technology. I gasp when I recall seeing the first aeroplane in 1911 looking like an apple crate propelled by an electric fan and the train ride across the continent in two nights and three days. And now five hours!

Such amazing achievements have been enough to engender euphoric hopes and to shatter the deterministic analogies of the orbits of the planets, the sequence of the seasons and the stages in the life of man. The gains in science and technology suggested the possibility of equal advance in the social field. Such was the dream of Condorcet and Spenser. And in the realm of spirit man could scale the mystic's ladder of purification, illumination, and unification. These fitted well the scheme of Hegel. Purification was for him the overcoming of the passions. Illumination was self-knowledge, and unification was the merging of the spirit with freedom and truth. The culmination was to be achieved by that profoundest of all peoples, the German nation.[23]

An element of determinism supportive of advance was introduced by the doctrine of organic evolution, which itself moved from the descent of man from lower forms to ascent toward the higher. Newman Smythe and Teilhard de Chardin projected the culmination beyond the frontier of death and for that matter the Catholic doctrine of purgatory has long since provided the possibility of moral progress after the end of history. The Marxists have combined the idea of progress with a dynamism destined inevitably to establish the classless society.

For the most part the ideas of progress have looked to man rather than to God to bring it to pass. Education would shape the public mind and one gain would open the way for another. God might be directing the process but divine interventions in history were not demonstrable in the past nor to be expected in the future. At the same time there was a religious concept of progress in the sense of a better time to come in the Jewish-Christian apocalypticism and millenarianism, often connected with messianism.[24] The new era would be inaugurated by a heroic divinely inspired leader, a messiah. A wave of apocalypticism swept over Judaism after the Babylonian exile and the Roman occupation. The mood passed over into Christianity and focused on the person of Jesus, who proclaimed the advent of the kingdom of God, present already in a measure and to be realized in fulness with the coming of the Son of Man. The early church identified Jesus with this figure and awaited his speedy return.

When the coming was delayed the date was from time to time advanced. Augustine postponed the return indefinitely because with the Lord a day is as a thousand years and a thousand years as a day.

In the late eleventh century the sense of immediacy was revived by Joachim of Fiore. The scheme of calculation was based on the 1260 days spent in the wilderness by the woman in the book of Revelation. These days were taken to be years. When nothing happened in 1260 this figure was added to some date in the early period of the church such as to bring the time just ahead of the period of the calculator. In the sixteenth century if one added to the Council of Nicea in 325 one arrived at 1585, and so on up to our own day.

Curiously both the secular idea of progress through the hand of man and the religious through the intervention of God were in a sense retrogressive, looking for advance through the recovery of a one time idyllic age. In Greek literature the myth of the golden age is found in the poem of Hesiod, who portrayed the age of gold, marked by ease, prosperity and peace, followed successively by the ages of silver and bronze to the age of iron, wherein families were at odds, oaths violated, and might was right. Aratus, the Stoic, declared that already in the age of bronze the sword was forged and justice fled to dwell among the stars. At Rome, Ovid indulged in nostalgic verses on the Hesiodic idyll when, without moats, cities were secure. Virgil combined Greek primitivism, Roman imperialism, and Hebrew messianism. Even before the accession of Augustus the poet announced that a child would be born at whose coming a race would descend from heaven to restore the age of gold. The Hebrew parallel was that the bliss of Eden would be restored in the messianic age; the bow would be broken, the spear cut in sunder, the chariot burned in the fire, and the wilderness would be as Eden and the desert like the garden of the Lord.[25]

The Renaissance looked to a past better documented. The glory that was Greece and the grandeur that was Rome were to be revived. The Latin language, corrupted during the Middle Ages, should be restored to the vocabulary of Cicero and the silver age. The reform movements in Christendom have all harked back to Christian beginnings, assuming an intervening fall. For Luther the fall consisted in the rise of the temporal power of the papacy, for the Catholics in the emergence of heresy, for the Anabaptists in the union of church and state under Constantine. The Romantic movement looked to the *bon sauvage,* who in America became Hiawatha or the Mohican. Some early in our century turned to Asia for the unspoiled man. Witness Lowes Dickinson's *Letters of John Chinaman.* The strength of these theories lies in the belief that if man was once capable of an age of gold, he may be so again. The disappointing point is that the fall also may recur.

A puzzling point is to know why both secular and religious concepts of progress shifted at times in the modern period from gradualism to violence. The secular view looked to the power of education, the apocalyptic to the unaided arm of the Lord. Circumstance may explain the shift; frustration over delay, plus an emergent possibility of success through force. The biblically minded, and of such were most Europeans well into the nineteenth century, were inhibited by the parable of the tares in which the servants asked the master whether they should root out the weeds among the wheat.[26] They were told to wait till the harvest when the reapers would do the weeding. In the gospel the reapers were the angels. This offered a way out. Thomas Müntzer in the sixteenth century declared that "The angels who sharpen their sickles are the earnest servants of God who carry out the zeal of divine wisdom." [27] In the Puritan struggle a century later, Stephen Marshall declared parliament to be the angel.[28]

In our day the idea of progress is no longer in vogue.[29] The discoveries of science and the inventions of technology have furnished the tools for the contemporary holocausts of cynical brutality. Some feel that in the moral realm we have made no advance over antiquity. A comparison of past and present is in order, though the evidence affords no conclusive answer.

Certainly in antiquity brutality abounded. The normal practice was the enslavement of a conquered population. Crucifixion was the punishment for non-Romans. Gladiatorial combats were the rage. Sadistic brutality is reported of Phalaris, the tyrant of Syracuse, who is said to have burned his victims inside a brazen bull that their cries might bellow through the mouth.[30] War is always brutal. Aeschylus describes it in his day:

> Groaning within: without
> A net is spread,
> Gripping the towers about.
> Man strikes man dead;
> And inarticulately
> Like beasts in dread,
> Mother and infant cry,
> And blood runs red.
> Running they rob, they fly.[31]

Athens wiped out the population of the island of Melos because of refusal to be neutral instead of her ally.[32] Tacitus reports the strictures of the Britons that "The Romans are robbers of the world. After denuding the land, they rifle the sea. They are rapacious toward the rich and domineering toward the poor, satiated neither by the East nor by the West. Pillage, massacre and plunder they grace with the name of empire and where they make a desert call it peace." [33] Orosius the Spaniard considered the ravages of the Goths in the early fourth century to be but flea bites compared to the Roman conquest of Spain when the natives killed their wives and children and cut their own throats rather than linger amid carnage and famine.[34] The conquered Greeks complained, "What manner of men are the Romans? Are they not shepherds who, unable because of base blood to secure wives, seized them by violence? who established their city by parricide and sprinkled the foundation of their walls with the blood of a brother?" [35] Horace, as we have noted, saw a virus of corruption in the Roman bloodstream because the city had been founded on the fratricide of Remus by Romulus.[36]

On the other hand the stories of barbarism in antiquity may have been the exaggerations of detractors. The Greeks portrayed the Assyrian Sardanopolus (Asurbanipal) as an utterly degenerate effeminate roué. But the inscriptions of his reign prove him to have been a remarkable sovereign who brought Assyria to her peak.[37] Again there is the case of Alexander. Diodorus Siculus records that when the city of Tyre resisted his efforts to advance the unity of mankind by merging the Greeks and the Persians, he punished the city by hanging or crucifying 2,000. And in the silver age of Latin literature Alexander fared badly. Seneca compared him to a beast rending more than he could devour,[38] and Quintius Curtius had a Scythian ambassador tell Alexander that he who boasted to have come against brigands was himself a brigand. [39] Yet that very same Diodorus, who tells of the massacre in Tyre, describes Alexander on other occasions as benign. A modern editor thinks he combined two divergent sources which he did not bother to harmonize.[40] Is there not the possibility that Alexander was both brutal and benign?

The religion of ancient Israel could accommodate both attitudes. In the thirteenth chapter of Deuteronomy we read that if in any of the cities occupied by the Hebrews "certain base fellows seduce the people into worshiping other gods, the inhabitants of that city, including the cattle, shall be put to the edge of the sword," whereas the Book of Jonah calls for compassion on that great city of Nineveh.

Men can be beasts. Men can be saints and we should not fail to do justice to the pagan saints: Socrates drinking the hemlock; Arria the wife of Paetus Thrasea, who when Nero sent word to her husband to commit suicide, plunged the dagger into her own breast and, handing it to him, said, "Paetus, it does not hurt."[41]

Regulus was the standard example of good faith. A prisoner at Carthage, he was released on oath to return that he might plead with the Roman senate to grant peace. Instead he urged war, and returned to be rolled over a cliff in a spiked barrel, though this detail may be legendary.[42] There was Musonius, the Stoic, who in a civil war went between the ranks pleading with the troops to refrain from this madness in which unwittingly a son had killed his father.[43]

Having thus essayed to balance the ill and the good in the ancient world let us now turn to our own. If we no longer have chattel slavery, what of the forced labor of millions of citizens inflicted by Stalin and Mao? Where in antiquity do we find genocide practiced on such a scale as in our holocausts? We no longer take infants by the heels and dash their brains against the stones. Instead we rain fire from the clouds and incinerate whole cities. As for torture, we refine by technology the methods of antiquity.

Listen to this report by American visitors to the tiger cages in Vietnam. "The cages were small stone compartments which seemed not quite five feet across and about nine feet long. There were three prisoners in each cage. The men walked up a stairway and looked down at the prisoners below the bars. The prisoners stared up. Not one could rise to his feet. . . . The prisoners were usually bolted to the floor, handcuffed to a bar or rod, or put in leg irons with the chain around a bar or rod. It did not take very long to ruin the legs, to bring partial or complete paralysis. . . . Each cage for the women held five, who ranged in age from fifteen to seventy. Nearly all had sores on their faces and bodies. One of the women pulled herself up to the side of the cage and called up to the guards, telling them how cruel they were. She was very short of breath but kept on. There was one guard, she said, who urinated on them." [44]

In the literature of antiquity I have encountered nothing so filthy.

In a way even more disconcerting is the discovery that our technology can be appropriated by the jungle. Listen to this:

> In 1963 in Brazil, as the Cintas Lagas tribe gathered for a funeral ritual, a small plane suddenly flew overhead and dropped small objects on the gathered tribe. The natives fled into the jungle, but the plane had dropped only packets of sugar, and soon they were all back in the clearing tasting the strange new chemical. Then the plane returned, and, having them all now in the open, bombed them to extinction. "No one has ever been able to find out how many Indians were killed because the bodies were buried in the bank." [45]

Now let us look at the better side. Crucifixion is gone. Gladiatorial combats are gone. So also is duelling. The ruthlessness attributed to Alexander is gone as well as the fanaticism of those who would wipe out a village of idolators. Slavery was abolished early in the last century, peaceably by England and somewhat later by a frightful war in the United States. The civil rights movement in our land, though not yet fully complete, has made enormous strides. A very significant point is that this advance has not been extorted by revolution or economic pressure but has been the work of the Christian conscience. The same is true of the recent purges in our political structure.

Another significant advance is that England relinquished her empire without compulsion. The reason was in part that she had brought the scions of the occupied lands to her universities where they imbibed the ideals of freedom and independence. Nations in general today are readier to help each other than in antiquity. The reason is in part to win allies. Still benevolence is not wholly lacking and private giving has been vast.

Religious liberty has been achieved in the western world. The process has been lamentably slow. The best arguments were voiced in the sixteenth century and not fully practiced until the nineteenth. Social change is all too slow and gains are not necessarily permanent. The two most tolerant countries in the age of the Reformation were Poland and Transylvania but the gains were swept away after a century.

Then we come to Christianity. Has it not changed human nature? Auerbach made a very significant comment on Peter's denial of his Master. Jesus had predicted that before the crowing of the cock there would be threefold denial. And when the cock crowed Peter went out and wept bitterly. No author in classical antiquity would have regarded the penitence of a peasant as other than a joke. Christianity turned it into a tragedy.[46] Julian the Apostate testified that the philanthropy of the Christians exceeded that of the pagans.[47] In seventeenth century England, when church and state were too impoverished to relieve the poor, the London merchants, who were mostly Puritans, stepped in.[48] The ideal of Christianity was not aggrandizement and power, but love and sacrifice. The Apostle Paul said, "It is no longer I who live, but Christ who lives in me." [49] And today when atrocities are committed they are viewed with horror rather than with a shrug.

Gain and loss, loss and gain confront us in the course of recorded history. Some evils have been corrected. New evils emerge. One can scarcely discover evidence of a fundamental change over the centuries in the nature of man.

Can there ever be such a change? Certainly yes with respect to behavior and with respect also to nature. Conversion can do it. We have just noticed the revolution in values implicit in the gospel account of Peter's denial. Repeatedly in Christian history the sinner has become the saint, the persecutor of a cause has come to be its advocate and even its martyr. But conversion has scarcely gone beyond the creation of a monastic order or a sect. An entire culture has never been profoundly converted.

Education can do it by instilling ideals which determine actions but education is incredibly slow. It is obviously more than the imparting of information. It must instill a nobler set of values. "Line upon line. Precept upon precept" and example upon example mark the course of educational advance. And how evanescent are the gains if a new crisis emerges!

Another way is brainwashing, an incessant din of admonition in the press or on the air with exclusion of everything contrary. It is the method of dictators and they have swayed multitudes. Yet one may rightly question whether they have done more than alter behavior. I recall that when in 1948 my wife and I were engaged for the Quakers in visitation in Germany I met a colleague who prior to the American entry into the war could not dare to write to an American unless unbeknownst to his son who would denounce him to the Gestapo. Now that very son greeted us and later went on a scholarship to Chicago. Such a *volte face* was a radical change in behavior. Was it also a change in human nature?

But it certainly is possible to change human nature by altering the body so that rationality, memory, and integrity vanish. Drugs, shock, constant exposure to intense light, induced sleeplessness, can so break a man that he is not the same person. That is why Cardinal Mindzenty on his arrest said that if he were to issue a confession not a word of it should be believed. He did not mean that it would be faked or forged. It would be a confession written and signed in his own hand, but he would not be the same Mindzenty.

The new medical technology offers us alike hope and dread. Drugs will relieve mental disorders. Tranquilizers compose uncontrollable feelings. Drugs will correct the chemical imbalance of schizophrenia. The new technology can change sex, breed babies in test tubes and produce genetic geniuses and morons. Such tampering with the body is frightening.[50]

And this raises the question of the morality of progress in science and invention. I once had a discussion with a notable inventor who insisted that the scientist has no responsibility other than to increase knowledge. The responsibility for its use rests with the technician. I asked whether he would be willing to engage in research for the improvement of germ warfare. He said he would for the United States, because our government could be trusted not to make an immoral use of it, but for Russia he would not. I told him he had given away his case. He acknowledged a point at which to halt. The scientist and the technician all have a responsibility for changes in the nature of man.

History thus far exhibits in man sublimity and baseness, self-sacrifice and "readiness to wade through slaughter to a throne and shut the gates of mercy on mankind." There are those who will walk into the fiery furnace and those who will chuckle over the torments of the damned. And let it not be forgotten that the angel and the ape make their abode in the same individual. Ours to hope, pray and labor for a loftier race.

Patterns in History

The theories of history thus far considered have led to qualified judgments: not cycles but rhythms, not inevitable progress but limited improvements. Now I would like to call attention to some patterns involving frequently certain sequences. They may be called the failures of success and the successes of failure.

The failures of success are of two kinds. The one does not entail the loss of the goal attained so much as an undesired and often unforeseen concomitant. In the physical area we split the atom and have then the problem of the disposal of the waste. We construct a nuclear plant and if the heated water is sent into the ocean we destroy the fish. In the biological field we develop an insecticide which disposes of moths but also of bees. In the animal kingdom we kill the wolves in Yosemite Park and then in the fall have to shoot the deer lest they die of hunger in the winter. India kills snakes and is overrun with rats. On the human level improved medicine reduces infant mortality and increases longevity, thereby increasing overpopulation. Our highways facilitate travel at the cost of deaths on the road, pollution of the air, and disfiguring of the countryside. The marvelous telephone enables me in no more time than for a local call to contact a son in California and a daughter in Alaska. Yet this wonderful invention has killed the art of letter-writing.

The moral, of course, is not to discontinue valid improvements but to anticipate with utmost care their possible adverse effects and if nevertheless they result, to devise rectifications.

The second type of failure is that in which the success destroys the goal achieved. One of the explanations offered for the fall of Rome is overextension. The frontiers were rounded out to the wall of Hadrian in Scotland and to Dura on the Euphrates. The empire was then too large for a central administration. We'll look at this again in another section. At any rate growth may dilute quality and destroy itself. This is notably the case in religious movements. The goal is to increase the number of genuine converts but augmenting numbers often brings in the unworthy. Sebastian Castellio put it well in the sixteenth century when he said that "one who forces people into the church is like a man who, to augment the wine, fills the barrel with water. He has more—but what's it like?"[51] Unavoidably the expansion of the church requires accommodation to the modes and mores of the people to be converted. When they enter they bring with them their past. An amalgation occurs which may be an enrichment, though more often a perversion. The saints become the successors of the gods and acquire some of their attributes.

Mere numbers wreck the ideal, even though the individuals are uncorrupted. St. Francis could manage with begging for only one day at a time so long as there were no more than a dozen holy vagabonds. But when the number reached five hundred, begging had to be specialized with solicitation assigned to the more successful beggars and at length the church assumed the onus of ownership, while allowing to the Franciscans the fruits. Then ensued splits in the order.

In our own day a minister told me he regretted having so

built up his congregation that he was never able to go to bed
without leaving a dozen imperative calls unmade. Several of my
students, after a decade in the parish, have resigned because the
load of counseling had become completely unmanageable. All of
this is not to say that the church should not increase in numbers.
There are ways of handling the problem. It has been done in
Korea. In Seoul there is a Presbyterian church with 9,000 members. The sanctuary seats 3,000. On a Sunday it is crowded three
times over. The ministerial staff numbers around twenty. The
city is divided into districts and the districts into cells of about
a dozen close enough to each other for weekly meetings.

That wealth corrupts is notorious. The Cistercian monk Cae-
sarius of Heisterbach, described the course of the monastic orders
in this sequence: Piety begets industry. Industry begets wealth.
Wealth disintegrates piety and piety in its fall dissipates wealth.[52]
The sequence then repeats itself. The Franciscan answer, as we
noted, was to have no wealth and live on alms. But the one who
gives alms must have wealth. If, then, wealth necessarily corrupts, the donor must suffer corruption that the Franciscans may
be uncorrupted. In the third century of our era the problem was
faced by Clement of Alexandria in his tract "Can a rich man
be saved?" The answer was yes if the wealth were devoted to
philanthropy.

That power corrupts has become a proverb. The history of the
church provides abundant illustrations. In the age of Constantine, the church did not deliberately seek power, but the emperor
believed the bishops in the administration of justice would be
incorruptible and gave status to their courts. Wealth confers
power and the church became wealthy by reason of donations
to be used for charity. When then in the sixth and seventh centuries the emperor at Constantinople was unable to ransom
prisoners from the barbarian invaders, the church took over,

even to the point of exercising the political role of making treaties. In the Middle Ages, the craving for power merged with idealism. If the church were able to arbitrate and direct the varied states, Europe would be brought closer to the kingdom of God. The Gregorian reform exalted the papacy above the secular rulers and Innocent III in the thirteenth century came closer than any before or since to being the arbiter of Europe. But the very process of manipulation so enmeshed the church in political tangles that by the time of the Renaissance the papacy was on the verge of becoming a secularized Italian city-state.

Even more striking are the successes of failure. None is more impressive than the crucifixion of Christ. In the eyes of the world it was a failure. Momentarily it seemed so to Christ himself. "My God, my God, why hast Thou forsaken me?" But the cross on which he died has become the symbol of a religion which has sustained millions. This is not to say that every cross will be a success in the achievement of an external goal. Many of the crucified have simply disappeared. The cross is not a club to overcome an opponent by an appeal to human sympathy. It is a witness to faith and may or may not have a social impact.

Turning now to the failures of empires, we must distinguish between an empire, a civilization, and a culture. An empire may fall and a civilization survive. A civilization may collapse and a culture be transmitted. Rome in the west disintegrated and having already herself absorbed the culture of the Greeks, transmitted it to the modern world. I was amazed when I visited the abbey of Corbie, constructed in A.D. 844 by Louis the Pious, to see on the wall of the imperial chamber a fresco of the fight of Ulysses with Scylla.

The disintegration of the British Empire was a failure so far as empire was concerned. My English uncle used to groan, "England's day is done." Might he not better have said "begun"? We have already remarked, as an indication of progress, her transition from empire to commonwealth without a revolution. One may add that her language has become the medium of communication between diverse linguistic groups. At Bangalore Seminary I found twenty-two languages on the campus and the kindergarten children had to play in English. The empire is gone. The legacy has been given to the world.

Another success of failure is the enforced migration of peoples. Expulsion from one's hearth bespeaks a failure somewhere. But the refugee often gains from the exile and the host may be incalculably benefitted. Witness the dispersion of the Huguenots to Berlin, England, Ireland, the United States and South Africa. Holland profited from the Calvinist refugees expelled from what is now Belgium. The Dutch exiles in sixteenth-century England stimulated her economic development. The Italian heretics enriched Poland. The refugees from Hitler and Mussolini have vastly enhanced American culture. Minorities, unable or unwilling to assimilate, have given an impetus to commerce as well as to culture. One thinks of the Jews and the Armenians.[53]

Causation

Causation in history is important for prediction. To this day we hear the forecast that America, by repeating the vices of ancient Rome, is headed for the dogs. America may indeed go to the dogs, but not to the same dogs and not in the same way. A brief survey of the multiple causes of the collapse of the Roman empire discloses great complexity and the extreme unlikelihood that the same concatenation of circumstances will recur.

At the outset some distinctions must be recognized in the ancient situation. The city of Rome did not constitute the empire, nor the empire the culture. A further point of great importance is that the empire comprised an eastern and a western half. Only the West collapsed. The East survived for another thousand years. Some say that it might as well have been dead, because it was moribund. Such was the thesis of Gibbon,[54] of late abundantly refuted by the Byzantine historians. Since, then, the East outlived the West by a millenium, any reasons adduced for the collapse of the West are irrelevant if equally applicable to the East.

The causes argued for the collapse are sometimes external, that is, beyond the control of the inhabitants. Among these one may first notice disease. W. H. S. Jones gave evidence that Greece was debilitated by malaria as far back as the beginning of the fifth century B.C.[55] He suggested that the debility explains why Greece succumbed first to Macedon and then to Rome. But at the same time he shows that malaria became widespread also in Rome, beginning early in the third century B.C. If, then, Greece was too weak to withstand Rome, why was Rome not too weak to overcome Greece? Zinsser has made the broader generalization that the lords of history are rats and lice.[56] He called especial attention to the plague which in A.D. 250 ranged from Egypt to Scotland and suggested a causal connection in that "it would have been impossible to maintain permanently a political and social organization of the type and magnitude of Rome in face of the lack of modern sanitary knowledge." There is a failure here to observe that following the epidemic of A.D. 250, the empire experienced a great resurgence through reforms of Diocletian.[57] In any case were rats, lice, fleas, and mosquitoes more vigorous in the West than in the East? A basic difficulty is, of course, the lack of reliable statistics on the degree of depopulation. If, however, the deficiency was a cause of the collapse in the fifth century, why not in the first, when Augustus penalized bachelors for being childless?

The influence of climate on civilization has been stressed by Ellsworth Huntington[58] who picked up Jones' theory of malaria and asked, "Why malaria?" Because of the change of climate, he answered. Rainfall diminished and flowing streams turned into stagnant pools, breeding malaria. But how does he know that rainfall diminished? Two lines of evidence are given. The first is the correspondence during the period of recorded precipitation between Southern California and the Mediterranean area. For Southern California the fall of rain can be traced back 2000 years by means of the rings of the sequoia trees. With this data transferred to the Mediterranean he would trace the ups and downs of Roman fortunes. But can we assume that the coincidence between the Mediterranean and Southern California has been a constant for two millenia? A second line of evidence is that the present supply of water would have been inadequate for the ancient cities. But how much water did they use? There were no flush toilets or hydrants. Was the supply more abundant in the East than in the West? There was, however, one significant climactic difference. On December 31 of the year 406 the Vandals, Alani, and Suevi invaded the western empire by crossing the Rhine on *ice*.[59] An army never invaded Byzantium by crossing the Bosporus on ice. The water was salt.

A further external explanation is an increased pressure from barbarian invaders. Ammianus Marcellinus, writing around A.D. 390, said that the Scythians had been kept from expansion to the south when the Chinese constructed a wall.[60] Thwarted to the south they pushed to the west and drove other barbarians over the rivers. Byzantium withstood the onslaught protected by the Bosporus, whereas, once the Danube and the Rhine were crossed, no natural barrier impeded the way to the sea. There is a point here.[61]

Another cause adduced is overextension,[62] an example, as already noted, of the failure of success. When the frontiers ran from Scotland to the Euphrates the area was too large to administer. Even in the sixteenth century Erasmus still thought so. How, he asked, can an emperor at Constantinople know what's going on in Ethiopia or on the Ganges? [63] True enough, but might not the division into East and West have sufficiently reduced the problem? More on that point in a moment.

A variant of the theme of overextension shifts from size to attitudes. The claim is that the incorporation of so many peoples eroded local loyalties. When, in 212, Caracalla conferred citizenship on all inhabitants of the empire the diverse populace from the Basques and the Berbers to the Syrians and the Egyptians no longer felt the passionate devotion of the embattled farmers who made the city of Rome the lord of Latium.[64] Still another point is that the universalizing of citizenship undercut the incentive to enter the army in order to obtain it.

Among other internal causes espoused are vice, slavery, and Christianity. Vice comprised luxury, debauchery, indolence, the pursuit of pleasure, and sex without babies. The Roman peace relieved the populace of the need for discipline to defend their walls and they succumbed to the *vitia pacis,* the vices of peace. Again the peace made possible the mingling of the constituent peoples of the empire, who, deracinated from their traditional environments, were emancipated from their ancestral mores. Tacitus spoke of Rome as the place where "all things base and abominable flow together and are celebrated." [65] The sturdy virtues of ancient agricultural Rome were eroded by urbanization. For the city of Rome such charges can be documented, but as an explanation of the political collapse of the empire in the fifth century the argument founders on chronology. The testimony regarding Roman decadence goes back to Sallust, Ovid, Tacitus and others of the centuries immediately before and after the birth of Christ. Why was vice so long in taking effect, and again, was Rome worse than Constantinople?

Then we have slavery to which as a cause the same objection applies, seeing that during the four hundred years leading up to the political collapse slavery actually improved.[66] The worst period was that of the inauguration of the Roman peace which terminated the victories, yielding hordes of captives to be enslaved. When the supply dried up, the treatment had to be improved. Slaves could no longer be driven to death and easily replaced. Future slaves had to be bred and family relations between slaves respected. As an incentive to better work, slaves were allowed to acquire property with which in time to purchase freedom. Important functions were performed by slaves, and high offices held by the half-emancipated freedmen. In the second century an ex-slave became the bishop of Rome. When Alaric took Rome in A.D. 410, slaves were better off than under Augustus.

Christianity was blamed by Gibbon as a partial cause of the collapse because otherworldliness and asceticism undercut civic duty and loyalty. This might have happened. The Emperor Julian jeered that Christianity was no religion for an empire. Was the city of Alexandria, he scoffed, nurtured on the precepts of the Galilean? [67] But by the time of the barbarian invasions neither Ambrose, nor Augustine, nor the Christian populace declined to participate in the defense of the empire.

A recent writer would regard much of the previous discussion as beside the point because to his mind the "fall of Rome" was a myth.[68] He recognizes, of course, that centralized government in the West was succeeded by barbarian kingdoms. His point is rather that the transition was not so much a crash as a gradual process. The capture of Rome by Alaric was more of an emotional shock than a political convulsion. By that time Rome had long since been overshadowed by the new capital in the East and the frontier cities of Trier, Milan, Sirmium, and Sardica. The bishop of Rome was coming to be of greater influence than the envoy of the emperor. One might say that the fall of Rome in one sense was the rise of Rome in another.

The historian is perfectly right that the process was gradual. The barbarians had been infiltrating for centuries. The Roman government enlisted them in the army to fight other barbarians and thus relieve citizens of military service. Veterans were rewarded with plots of land on which they settled. More significantly, in the period leading up to the fall, the barbarians were admitted in vast numbers *with their families.* We have records of settlements within the empire under Augustus of 50,000, under Tiberius of 40,000, under Nero of more than 100,000, under Constantine of 300,000 and under Theodosius of 200,000.[69] One might almost say that the "fall" of Rome was a case of the breakdown of controlled immigration.

Two significant differences between East and West are demonstrable. One is geographical, the other psychological. As for geography, the East, having lost the Levant and Egypt to the Saracens—another success of failure—became thereby a compassable territory solidified by a common language, Greek, and a common religion, orthodoxy. The West, on the other hand, was segmented by natural boundaries. Africa was cut off from Europe by the sea, England from the continent by the channel, the Pyrenees separated Spain from Gaul, and the Alps Gaul from Italy. There were linguistic differences. Punic survived in Africa, Basque continues to this day in Spain, and Celtic was long in use in Normandy. As for religion, though Christianity prevailed, paganism still had such strength that Augustine had to compose the fears of Christians that the pagans might be right in claiming the present disasters to be due to the displeasure of the gods over the spread of the new faith.

The other difference had to do with the attitude toward the barbarians on the part of the inhabitants of the empire. The East became hostile after Theodosius permitted 200,000 Visigoths to settle in the empire following the defeat at Adrianople in 378. The native resentment was voiced by Synesius of Cyrene in his address to Arcadius, the son and successor of Theodosius. "Wolves, though they be but whelps, should not be allowed among the sheep." The "ill omened dogs" (a phrase from Homer) should be reduced to the status of helots or driven from the land. A native army attacked a barbarian contingent under Gainas and slew 3,500.[70] Thereafter the empire returned to the system of native-born troops.

Not so in the West. There the Roman general Stilicho, himself of German descent, twice let slip an opportunity to crush Alaric who in 410 took Rome. Evidently Stilicho was not so opposed to infiltration. As for the attitude of the populace to the invaders we have a few examples markedly different from the stance of Synesius. Augustine, speaking for northern Africa, gave the invaders credit for sparing those who took refuge in churches, whether Christians or pagans.[71] Orosius, the Spaniard, considered the ravages of the Goths but fleabites in comparison with the atrocities committed by the Romans in the conquest of Spain, when natives killed their wives and children and flung themselves over cliffs rather than linger amid carnage and famine.[72] Salvian in Gaul claimed that the barbarians were more chaste than the Romans and lauded Gaisaric the Vandal for closing the brothels of Carthage.[73] From these few items too much is not to be inferred as to popular feeling, but the difference between the statements is striking.

The sum of the matter is that causation is exceedingly difficult to assess. One can do no more than offer a plausible conjecture. That being so, the past affords no warrant for precise predictions. The future is open and we have a chance. The same conclusion follows from what we have observed as to the variables in human behavior and diversity of patterns.

God in History

Thus far we have dealt with the theories of history without introducing the hand of God. All such theories are susceptible of a religious interpretation and their authors almost without exception have been believers. The cyclical view may assume that God raises up and casts down. The progressive may picture man as cooperating with God. The pattern of the failure of success fits the story of the rich man who crammed his barns only to be told, "Fool, this night your soul is required of you." [74] The success of failure accords with the text that "except a grain of wheat falls into the earth and dies it remains alone, but if it dies it bears much fruit." [75] The capricious appears such only in the eyes of man, while behind the apparently fortuitous lies the finger of God. The meaning of history is not plumbed without consideration of whether it is directed by God, whether it throws light on the nature of man and God, and whether God invests with meaning the historical enigmas.

The relationship of God and history involves the concept of time. For Augustine the only real time is the present since the past is memory and the future hope. Yet he saw connections. Endeavor in the present is inspired by hope, guided by memory and sustained by faith in the God who marks the sparrow's fall. Those theologies that conceive of God as the ground of being, the cloud of unknowing, the god beyond theism, tend to dissolve time into eternity. But those theologies that conceive of God as participating in the historical process by acts now of wrath, now of mercy are confronted by grave problems because not a little of what happens in history appears incongruous with love and justice.

The course of events presents both iniquity and inequity. With respect to God iniquity is the more readily disposed. For, according to the process theologians God has bestowed upon man the gift of freedom. Man has abused the gift through sin. God cannot prevent man from sinning without withdrawing the gift. Consequently man bears the responsibility and God is exonerated.

The problem of inequity is more troublesome. At one time it was a prime concern of Christian thinkers because the inequities of life were projected into eternity. God ordained prior to birth some to everlasting bliss and some to everlasting woe. Luther confessed that by this contemplation he had more than once been cast down to the abyss of utter desolation.[76] The doctrine appeared to him to be incontrovertibly biblical because Pharaoh was declared in Holy Writ to have been hardened in heart by an act of God. Jacob was foreordained to bliss and Esau to doom before ever the two were born. Calvin also shuddered and called predestination "the horrible decree," but faced it unflinchingly with the assertion that God is not the father of all, but only of the elect. The dilemma could be escaped by denying that predestination was either biblical or true, as Erasmus did, or by denying immortality. Both expedients are today in vogue.

But eliminating predestination from the life to come does not dispose of it in the life that now is. Calvin ruthlessly looked at the facts. "Whenever I see a moron," he said, "I think of what God might have made me." [77] Why does God suffer some to be born idiots and some geniuses? And this is by no means the only inequity of life.

Here we have precisely the problem of Job in more acute form because the inequities are in no way related to the worth of the individual. The Old Testament account gives a revolving picture of God who puts Job through excruciating trials simply to win a wager with Satan who asserts that the constancy of Job to which God points with pride would end in cursing were favors withdrawn. God then grants Satan leave to test Job by stripping him of all save life. The Sabaeans make off with his oxen and asses, leaving the servants slain. Fire descends from heaven to consume the sheep and the shepherds. The Chaldaeans steal the camels and put the servants to the edge of the sword, while a great wind from the wilderness shatters the house where his sons and daughters are feasting. They are dead. And Job says, "The Lord has given. The Lord has taken away. Blessed be the name of the Lord." And Job sinned not and charged not God with wrong.

"But let me touch his flesh," jibed Satan. And with God's consent Job is covered with hideous sores. His wife nags that he must have deserved it. His trial would have been less if she had died with the children. Three friends come to console him that the innocent are not afflicted. He must, then, not be innocent. Job roundly disclaims the charge. "When have I eaten my portion alone without succoring the fatherless? When have I let any perish for want of clothing and have not warmed him with the fleece of my sheep? If I have raised my hand against the fatherless may my shoulder blade fall from my shoulder and let my arm be broken from the socket. Why does the Almighty not hold court? Would that I knew where I might find him. Then would

I lay my case before him." God at length responds saying, "Who are you to chide me? Can you bind the chains of the Pleiades or loose the bands of Orion? Can you tilt the water skins of the heavens? Can you send forth lightnings? Did you give to the horse his might? Is it by your wisdom the hawk soars? Can you draw out Leviathan with a hook?" Job answers, "I uttered what I did not understand, things too wonderful for me which I did not know. Now mine eyes see thee. Therefore I despise myself and repent in dust and ashes."

One can readily, like Jung,[78] pour scorn upon the God of Job, forgetting that we have here simply a dramatization of the human condition. The innocent suffer alike with the guilty. "God sends his sun and his rain on the just and the unjust." [79] And his calamities upon the guiltless. Jesus saw it. "Do you think that these Galileans [whose blood Pilate mingled with their sacrifices] were worse sinners than all other Galileans, because they suffered thus? Or those eighteen upon whom the tower in Siloam fell and killed them, do you think that they were worse offenders than all the others who dwelt in Jerusalem? I tell you No." [80] In the case of the man born blind the question was, "Who sinned, this man or his parents?" And the answer was "Neither." [81]

Job's trials were of two kinds—disaster and disease. A tornado brought down the house upon his children. The utter lack of moral discrimination of such calamities long since troubled the pagans. Lucretius asked why Jupiter does not strike down criminals. Why are the guiltless consumed by tornado and fire? If Jove would guard us against his thunderbolts, why does he not let us know they are coming? Why does his bolt shatter temples and images of the gods? What of the fires that with such fury belched from the throat of Mt. Etna? [82]

Well might the ancients wonder why the eruption of Vesuvius took the life of Pliny the Elder, not to speak of burying Herculaneum and Pompei. Similarly Voltaire raged against the Lisbon earthquake, and recently in Guatemala a man standing before his demolished dwelling cried, *"O Dio porque?* (O God why?)"

The other trial visited upon Job was disease. This presents the same problem. Some maladies, to be sure, are brought on by moral delinquency, but most have no relationship to the worth of the sufferer and most notably is this true in the case of the elderly. Old Dr. Parker, the distinguished British preacher, used to say that nothing so troubled him as the suffering of God's aged saints.

Two explanations are offered to justify the ways of God to man. The first is that orderliness in the universe is better than caprice. The task of man is to discover the laws of that orderliness and to conform himself. In time his ingenuity will enable him to predict exactly when and where earthquakes will occur. Yes, but why should it take centuries to find out? And this applies equally to the discoveries which alleviate pain and cure disease. Why have so many been pocked or killed by smallpox prior to vaccination? Why have so many quaked with malaria before the discovery of the role of the mosquito? What of the men who have died of cancer of the groin before the prostate operation became feasible? Why was a ruptured appendix so often fatal prior to penicillin? If God desires to exercise our resourcefulness why is the way so arduous and so unfair to those who antedate the solutions? Job's loathsome sores might have been cleared by a few injections. And what of all the psychic disorders which afflict our generation and for which we do not understand the causes and the cures? Is there a chemical imbalance? Is there a genetic factor? Do childhood repressions warp the disposition? Are the strains of our society more than the most sensitive and gifted among us can bear? The inequity is here between the generations. *O Dio porque?*

Another answer is that disaster and evil are not altogether bad. Light requires darkness and the good needs the bad to show forth its excellence. Joy is greater after pain. Augustine describes seafarers caught in a raging storm. In terror they crouch as the waves batter the barque. When calm ensues how much greater the joy by reason of the anguish![83] The quality of mercy is enhanced by cruelty. The luster of virtue is better seen over against the repulsiveness of vice. The reply may well be a preference for a little less luster.

We are reminded that, if not vice, at any rate disasters and diseases have their blessings. Trials bring out heroism. Suffering makes saints. Virtue untried is flabby. The centuries of finding out how to avert adversities are a chapter in the training of man. Cold comfort!

A more subtle and frightful torment is the inescapable choice between two repugnant alternatives. The inequity here is between the sensitive, who are anguished and the callous, who are cynical. We have it in the story of Jephthah who swore an oath to the Lord that if he were given victory over the Amorites he would sacrifice as a burnt offering to the Lord "whoever on my return comes from the doors of my house to greet me." And the first to come forth with timbrels and dancing was his only child, his daughter.[84] The pagan parallel is the case of Agamenon and Iphigenia. Failure to keep the vow would bring the wrath of heaven upon the community.

Such dilemmas are recurrent throughout all history, however varied the form. The theme is pursued in Sartre's *Le Diable et le Bon Dieu (The Devil and the Good Lord)*. The people of Worms have rebelled against the exactions of their Lord, the archbishop, and are holding 200 priests as hostages whose lives will be forfeit if the demands are not met. A general, for his own reasons, would be willing to wipe out Worms and its 2000 inhabitants. There is a curé who has ministered to the poor of Worms and loves them. He is also a churchman and loves the church. The archbishop has the key to a tunnel giving access to Worms. He commits it to the curé with instructions to pass it on to the general. The curé is outraged. Never would he sacrifice the 2000 citizens to save the 200 priests. But the churchman in him triumphs. He delivers the key. The bishop in the meantime pardons the city and the general withdraws the siege. No one is killed, but the curé is so overwhelmed with remorse at having betrayed the poor of Worms that he lies about himself in order to be defrocked from the ministry of which he is unworthy.

This, though fiction, is no idle tale. How often has an idealist been called upon to sacrifice his family! Take John Bunyan in the Bedford jail while his blind wife Mary struggles to support the children. And he might have been free had he been willing to abandon his witness. The dictators play upon family devotion to silence dissidents by threats of reprisals on loved ones. And sometimes the choice is to know whom to help when all cannot be helped. Leonard Kenworthy was a Quaker in Nazi Germany until withdrawn by the American entry into the war. Up to that point he had the responsibility of deciding which Jews might take advantage of the limited immigration quota to the United States. He gave preference to those with dependents. A childless blind man taxed him with discrimination because of his blindness. The reproach rankles to this day.[85]

Another trial described in Scripture is more harrowing because the conflict is between all the impulses of the moral man and what is deemed to be a divine command. The classic case is Abraham's readiness to sacrifice Isaac. Luther felt intensely the excruciating trial of the father called upon to use the sacrificial knife on his son, but for him this did not present a problem because he assumed there would always be a ram in the thicket. The following, in condensed form, is his exposition.

Abraham was told by God that he must sacrifice the son of his old age by a miracle, the seed through whom he was to become the father of kings and of a great nation. Abraham turned pale. Not only would he lose his son, but God appeared to be a liar. He had said, "In Isaac shall be thy seed," but now he said, "Kill Isaac." Who would not hate a God so cruel and contradictory? How Abraham longed to talk it over with someone! Could he not tell Sarah? But he well knew that if he mentioned it to anyone he would be dissuaded and prevented from carrying out the behest. The spot designated for the sacrifice, Mount Moriah, was some distance away; "and Abraham rose up early in the morning, and saddled his ass, and took two of his young men with him, and Isaac his son, and clave the wood for the burnt-offering." Abraham did not leave the saddling of the ass to others. He himself laid on the beast the wood for the burnt offering. He was thinking all the time that these logs would consume his son, his hope of seed. With these very sticks that he was picking up the boy would be burned. In such a terrible case should he not take time to think it over? Could he not tell Sarah? With what inner tears he suffered! He girt the ass and was so absorbed he scarcely knew what he was doing.

He took two servants and Isaac his son. In that moment everything died in him: Sarah, his family, his home, Isaac. This is what it is to sit in sackcloth and ashes. If he had known that this was only a trial, he would not have been tried. Such is the nature of our trials that while they last we cannot see to the end. "Then on the third day Abraham lifted up his eyes, and saw the place afar off." What a battle he had endured in those three days! There Abraham left the servants and the ass, and he laid the wood upon Isaac and himself took the torch and the sacrificial knife. All the time he was thinking, "Isaac, if you knew, if your mother knew that you are to be sacrificed." "And they went both of them together." The whole world does not know what here took place. They two walked together. Who? The father and the dearest son—the one not knowing what was in store but ready to obey, the other certain that he must leave his son in ashes. Then said Isaac, "My father." And he said, "Yes, my son." And Isaac said, "Father, here is the fire and here the wood, but where is the lamb?" He called him father and was solicitous lest he had overlooked something, and Abraham said, "God himself will provide a lamb, my son."

When they were come to the mount, Abraham built the altar and laid on the wood, and then he was forced to tell Isaac. The boy was stupefied. He must have protested, "Have you forgotten: I am the son of Sarah by a miracle in her age, that I was promised and that through me you are to be the father of a great nation?" And Abraham must have answered that God would fulfill his promise even out of ashes. Then Abraham bound him and laid him upon the wood. The father raised his knife. The boy bared his throat. If God had slept an instant, the lad would have been dead. I could not have watched. I am not able in my thoughts to follow. The lad was as a sheep for the slaughter. Never in history was there such obedience, save only in Christ. But God was watching, and all the angels. The father raised his knife; the boy did not wince. The angel cried, "Abraham, Abraham!" See how divine majesty is at hand in the hour of death. We say, "In the midst of life we die." God answers, "Nay, in the midst of death we live."

Luther once read this story for family devotions. When he had finished, Katie said, "I do not believe it. God would not have treated his son like that."

"But, Katie," answered Luther, "he did." [86]

Luther's answer really did not meet her objection. God did not indeed intervene to prevent the crucifixion of Christ but neither did he command Pilate to decree the execution. Kierkegaard rightly saw that the situation was unique and devoted to it his *Fear and Trembling*. This was not a case like that of Jephthah and Agamemnon. God commanded Abraham to sacrifice his son without giving any reason whatsoever. Kierkegaard regarded obedience in such a case as superb. Rather it was appalling. Abraham should have defied God, should have affirmed that a God who would command a father to kill his son without a reason was a God not worthy to be worshiped. The trouble with Kierkegaard was his addiction to the late medieval concept of the omnipotence of God who can do absolutely anything. He can make black white, right wrong. He can annul the past so that a harlot would be a virgin. He could have become incarnate in a donkey or a pumpkin rather than in the man Christ Jesus. These were the assertions which revolted Erasmus who asserted that unless God imposes limits on omnipotence Christian morality is undercut.

The question came up again in his debate with Luther. Erasmus said that if God damns some and saves others before ever they are born, he is a tyrant. Luther retorted, "Who are you to judge God? Let God be God." And Erasmus reiterated, "Let God be good." Then he put another question to Luther. "How do you know that God has done this?" "Out of the Scripture," said Luther. "God hardened Pharaoh's heart." "O no. He just gave Pharaoh a chance to show how hard it was," rejoined Erasmus. "But before ever they were born," retorted Luther, "God said, 'Jacob have I loved. Esau have I hated.'" "That," said Erasmus, "was because he saw how they would turn out. How can you be so sure?"

That is the question Kierkegaard should have put to Abraham. How could he be so certain that God required of him the sacrifice of his son? This is no antiquated problem. The best analogy to the trial of Abraham is that of a conscientious objector to military service in a popular war. His choice is not between two repugnant acts, unless of course his refusal would mean defeat for those in the war. Normally his choice is between loyalty to God and loyalty to the state. How then does he know that his stand is the will of God? His plight is that of Luther who after his magnificent stand at Worms, when hidden in the castle of the Wartburg, would say to himself, "Are you alone wise?"

The war resister is similarly plagued. I remember when Jane Addams of the Hull House settlement in Chicago visited our Quaker equipe in France, she told us how hard it had been to keep assurance of the rightness of her stand when all of the friends she so esteemed were otherwise minded. This is the most acute trial, the necessity for decision with an ambiguous choice. And it is not a trial which God visits indiscriminately on the just and the unjust. It is precisely those whom we would call just who are so troubled. The majority fall in line with popular clamor, and experience no interior crisis.

Where then does all of this leave us with respect to God in history? Disaster, suffering, and sin are all there. Some among us invoke the devil, but they have still to ask why God in casting down Lucifer from heaven did not leave him powerless. For our age the devil is dead, while the demonic survives. If, then, there is any supernatural power behind life's calamities, the responsibility devolves on God.

Luther very clearly saw this and gave up on an answer in this present life. Some things, he said, we understand in the light of nature, some in the light of grace, some only in the light of glory. If God damns some and saves others before they are born he appears to be a tyrant. We are not to say that he is a tyrant. We do not see why not. There is the hidden God whose ways are past finding out and there is the revealed God. And how revealed? By Jesus Christ his only Son our Lord.

And what do we know about Jesus? He was born when a decree went out from Augustus Caesar, in time, in history. And thus to history our quest has brought us back.

The Jesus of History

Our discovery of the revelation of God in Jesus is not quite as simple as it was for Luther because he lived in the era prior to the quest for the historical Jesus and therefore assumed that the discourses of Jesus in John's gospel are the very words of the only begotten Son of God, whereas modern scholarship holds that the evangelist followed the common practice in antiquity of composing orations, speeches, and discourses deemed suitable for the subject. This is not to say that Jesus is not the water and the bread of life, but only that this is what the early Christians had found him to be rather than what he himself claimed. The distinction is of no great import if Christian experience validates the claim. But there are discrepancies of word and deed presenting difficulties.

Part of the problem lies in the abundance of material both as to the text and the interpretation of the New Testament. If only one manuscript of an ancient document is extant there can be no debate as to the correct readings but when, as in the New Testament, there are thousands of manuscripts with variant readings the determination of the authentic becomes a special discipline. With respect to interpretation, the four gospels and the epistles, though in essential accord, differ sufficiently to give rise to different theologies. They may be complementary, they may be contradictory.

Attention to the problems of text and interpretation were precipitated in large measure by developments in other fields. The invention of printing and the publication of the Bible in print necessitated decisions as to which manuscript or which readings from different manuscripts should be sent to the printer.

In the eighteenth century the problem shifted from the determination of the text to the reliability of the content. The trouble started when the apple fell on the head of Newton and convinced him of the immutable law of gravitation. If immutable, then Jesus could not have walked on water without going to the bottom. The concept of immutability was then extended to all the processes of nature and miracles were excluded in the sense of events incapable of repetition and verification in the present. Consequently Jesus could not have fed five thousand with five loaves and two fishes and could not have risen bodily from the tomb.

The apologists then explained the miracles as misunderstandings of natural events. They differed among themselves as to the nature of the misunderstandings. One perceives styles in the explanation of the three miracles: the walking on the water and stilling of the storm, the multiplying of the loaves and the resurrection.[87]

In the case of walking on water and stilling the storm, Jesus was standing in a haze on the shore. (Haze was the ultimate resource of the rationalists.) Jesus called to the disciples who were laboring in the boat. Peter, hearing the voice, dove into the shallow water and made for shore. The waves so buffeted him that he would have drowned had not Jesus reached out a hand

and pulled him to the beach. The two then boarded the boat which came into the lee of a mountain and the wind subsided.[88]

In the story of the loaves, Jesus is represented as having fed 5,000 with five loaves and two fishes. Twelve baskets were left over. One rationalistic version was that Jesus belonged to a clique of the Essenes, who on a mountain had a cave stored with bread. When the vast assembly gathered to hear Jesus was famished, he stood at the mouth of the cave, receiving loaves from confederates, which he passed on to the disciples for general distribution. Twelve baskets remained. A further version was that Jesus bade the multitude, rich and poor together, to sit on the green sward. He then blessed and brake the loaves and fishes in their sight and gave to the disciples. This example of sharing was infectious. The rich, who had brought lunches, shared with the poor. All were fed and twelve baskets remained.

With respect to the resurrection, all the rationalists were agreed that Jesus was never dead. Credence was given to this hypothesis because Pilate marvelled that he was so soon dead. As a matter of fact he was not. Paulus, the chief of the rationalists, said that he could not have been dead because, after appearing in the midst of the disciples, he was able to eat a fish. Paulus was parsimonious of details. Schleimacher was not.[89] Jesus, he said, was placed in the tomb. Unaware of this, someone rolled away the stone. Jesus emerged naked. Clothed by the gardener, he was assumed by Mary to be the gardener. The "risen" Christ was able to go through a closed door because someone, unbeknownst to the others, had turned the key. Jesus mingled secretly with only a few, lest his reappearance cause them danger. Other interpreters explained the resurrection as due to aromatic spices and still others as caused by the earthquake. One version had it that Joseph of Arimathea and Nicodemus went to Pilate and tried to bribe him to allow them to take Jesus down while still alive. Pilate, rejecting the bribe, willingly gave consent and was rewarded with a sweet kiss from his wife.

Strauss branded the explanations as more miraculous than the miracles.[90] He introduced the concept of myth, which is the concretion of an idea in the form of an episode, a story. The myth of the resurrection is to be rejected outright because there was no resurrection. A myth in that case is simply false. But in the case of walking on the water and quelling the storm, the raging sea represents death over which Jesus is the victor. The core idea in the miracle of the loaves is that Jesus is the bread of life. Accessory ideas are his connection with the past and the future. His act recapitulated the feeding of the Israelites in the wilderness by Moses and the multiplication of barley loaves by Elisha. In John's gospel the loaves multiplied by Jesus were of barley.[91] The future reference[92] was to the Eucharist and the love feast from which the remaining fragments were taken to the absent by the seven deacons.[93] In Mark's second account of the miracle the number of baskets was seven.

Strauss with his concept of myth opened a Pandora's box. What if the entire picture of Jesus were a myth? What if he never existed at all? A number of writers around the turn of the century were saying just this, though with varying slants.

Kalthoff, a parish minister, said that the idea expressed by the myth is that a religious movement originates with groups rather than with individuals.[94] In that case the Jesus myth was inappropriate because it centered on an individual.

Kautsky[95] held that the core of the myth was revolution, violent revolution. Jesus blessed the poor, cursed the rich, and said that he was not sent to bring peace but a sword.[96] Original Christianity was violent and, although the gospels are no more reliable than Homer, they do in spots disclose the original intent of the movement when they ascribe to Jesus the saying about bringing the sword and rightly report that Jesus was executed as a political rebel. Around his figure the myth was elaborated, though later toned down when the Christian community became more affluent.

For Drews the myth was the deification of humanity in general rather than concentrated in a single human being. "Man's consciousness of himself and of his true essence must itself be a divine consciousness." [97] To be rid of the individual focus is an emancipation.

The reply to these theories of non-existence pointed to the factual errors in the reconstructions. Christianity did not originate among the sullen jobless at Rome—the marks of a Palestinian origin are obvious—nor among a seething proletariate throughout the empire. The papyri of the common folk show no signs of massive discontent.[98] A further critique is that while all of the theorists construe the core of the myth in communal terms, all embody it in an individual.

The positive reply was that the New Testament contains a number of sayings and deeds of Jesus which went counter to the beliefs of the early Christian community and would never have been recorded if not actually true. Where obviously the same saying is reported in two sources, we are able to perceive the process of attenuation of the unpalatable.[99] Take for example the reply of Jesus when called "Good Master," that "none is good but God," which might be taken to mean that Jesus was neither good nor God. Mark obviates the difficulty by phrasing the question, "Why do you ask me about that which is good?" [100] Again when Jesus was called upon to prove his authority by a miracle, he answered, "This generation is an evil generation: it seeks a sign, but no sign shall be given except the sign of Jonah. For as Jonah was a sign to the men of Nineveh so will the Son of Man be to this generation." Matthew's gospel converts the refusal of a sign into the giving of the most stupendous of all signs, the resurrection, "for as Jonah was three days and three nights in the belly of the whale so shall the Son of Man be three days and three nights in the heart of the earth." [101] In the first three gospels we have the agonized prayer of Jesus in Gethsemane. "May this cup pass from me." Some early Christians saw here a sign of weakness and John's gospel reverses the meaning, for Jesus says, "Now is my soul troubled. And what shall I say, 'Father save me from this hour'? No, for this purpose have I come to this hour." [102]

Not only sayings but also episodes were troublesome for the early church. One was the baptism of Jesus by John whose baptism was for the remission of sins and Jesus was believed to have no sins. [103] John's gospel evades the problem by omitting the baptism. John the Baptist proclaims that one greater than he is coming and testifies to have seen the descent of a dove, but there is no baptism. [104] Again Jesus declares that there is none born of woman greater than John. [105] This unqualified praise was troublesome for the early church, confronted as it was by an independent sect of the followers of the Baptist, among whom had been Priscilla and Aquila. [106] We can understand then why the gospel writer would add to the superlative commendation of John the qualification, "Yet he who is least in the kingdom of heaven is greater than he."

There are other incidents which only an absolutely honest recorder would have mentioned, as that the mother and brothers of Jesus sought to lay hands on him because they believed him to be crazy. [107] A mythmaker would scarcely have concocted accounts of a denial by one disciple, betrayal by another, and desertion by all. Such admissions are the pillars of certainty. So much at least is true. From here we can build out. Whatever was troublesome for the early Christian community has the ring of authenticity.

Where we have two versions of the same saying we may be able to detect the original. But if there is only one version can we be sure that it is authentic? Some then have been disposed to say, "Does man's eternal salvation depend on what historians are able to demonstrate? The theory that Jesus did not exist passes over into the theory that it really does not matter whether or not he did. In 1911, Douglas Macintosh said that Christianity would never have arisen without belief in the existence of Jesus, but today could survive without it because the truths have been validated in Christian experience.[108] Frank Porter said that the ideal "comes to us as truth and works in us a saving and renewing power, through the gospel picture of Jesus Christ, not that the truth of the picture depends upon its historical actuality." [109] If I recall, he said to me that relinquishment of the belief in the historical actuality would bring a sense of loss.

In 1936, Paul Tillich said that even if Jesus never existed, yet for the Christian Christ is the center of history.[110] Presumably he meant the Christ idea. One should recall, however, that if for two thousand years Christ has been for Christians the center of history the reason is that they believed him to have existed. If they were mistaken, we have here the most colossal example of the power of an illusion to create a religion and a culture.

Not even for a Christian believer will the question of historicity down. Is there no difference between Christ and Hamlet? No one cares whether Hamlet was a historical person. He embodies a certain aspect of humanity. May we not also say the same of Christ? Is not the portrait sufficient without the subject? In that case one may well wonder whether we should keep the name Christian, since without Christ Christianity is either humanism or theosophy. Many values would indeed survive but the words placed by the fourth evangelist in the mouth of Jesus, "He that has seen me has seen the Father." [111] would have to be relinquished. There is significance for the understanding of God in the actual life of Jesus. The Word became flesh. The idea is not enough.

The question has not downed and some of the discarded theories still recur in modified form. The view of Kalthoff that attention should be centered on the early Christian community reappears not so much on the ground that a religion can arise only out of a community but rather because the community is the source of the only knowledge of which we can be sure. The quest for the historical Jesus is fruitless and we must seek rather to understand what the first Christians proclaimed about him. The word for proclamation is in Greek *kerygma*. Some go so far as to set this in opposition to the historic Jesus. Others maintain an essential unity.

The universalism of Drews reappears in the view that the ideals of Christianity are universal, whether or no embodied in the life of an individual. Kautsky's theory of the revolutionary origins of Christianity has been revamped by Brandon [112] who claims that Jesus himself was a rebel, a Zealot intent on liberating Israel from the yoke of Rome. Evidence is rightly adduced to show that some in Jesus' circle viewed him as a political messiah. Did not the angel say to Mary, "He shall sit upon the throne of his father David and of his kingdom there shall be no end"? James and John asked that they might sit on his left and right when he came in his kingdom. The disciples walking to Emmaus with the risen Lord, said, "We trusted that this was he who would deliver Israel." And prior to the ascension Jesus was asked, "Will you now restore the kingdom to Israel?" [113] There is no doubt that some entertained such expectations, but did Jesus? To claim that he did is to relegate the Sermon on the

Mount and related material to the end of the century as the work of Alexandrian Jews who never had approved of revolt in Israel. This is too drastic a revision.

Earlier threads are woven into a new pattern by Bultmann whose system is called "demythologizing."[114] He stands on the same base as the eighteenth-century rationalists who rejected in the New Testament all that was conceived in terms of the pre-scientific world view. Their solution was naturalistic explanations. That of Bultmann is flat rejection. Heaven and hell are not places. Demons and angels are not persons. And miracles in the sense of deviation from the orderly course of nature are to be rejected.

These affirmations are subsumed under the rubric of demythologizing. Myth, as we noted, is the concretion of an idea in the form of an episode, a story. There are two counts on which it is to be rejected. The first is if the idea itself is false. The resurrection in a physical sense is demythologized by denying that it ever happened. A second test is that a myth is acceptable only if there is no danger that it will be regarded as other than what it is. There are many embodiments of ideas in fictional form. Take *Moby Dick, Don Quixote, Alice in Wonderland,* Tolkien's Ring series and the tales of C. S. Lewis. They are delightful and helpful. But there are those who say that if Noah's ark is not actual fact, all Christianity goes by the board. In that case, Noah's ark is a dangerous myth. We must do our best to discover whether that which we are mythologizing is true.

We are back again then with history. Who was Jesus? What did he do? What did he say? There is no event in his career which has been deemed more crucial than the resurrection. An excursus is therefore in order as to its historicity.

The Meaning
of the Resurrection

Whereas the crucifixion is the most certain event in the career of Jesus, the resurrection is the least. The reason does not lie in a disparity of evidence. The resurrection is as fully attested as the crucifixion, but something which goes counter to universal human experience requires a great deal more by way of proof than that which happens every day. All die. Few if any return after death. Recent investigations have shown that some pronounced dead have been resuscitated. One is inclined to ask how long they were dead. For a time a chicken can run around with its head cut off. Have we evidence that anyone came back to life whose body, like that of Lazarus, stank? Or that anyone was raised "on the third day" like Jesus? Some reply, "We do not need such evidence. God can do anything." Yes, but did he? We cannot leap from what God can do to what he did. We must have evidence.

The testimony of the witnesses is weakened by reason of the credulity of the age to which they belonged. In the prescientific era skepticism was not rife as to the possibility of resurrections. The contemporaries of Jesus did not regard his resurrection as unique. They believed that he had raised three others: Jairus' daughter, the widow's son at Nain, and Lazarus. This does not weaken the case, some would say, because the God who raised up Jesus empowered him to raise also others. But one must then go a step further and point out that not only did Jesus have the power, but also Peter who raised Tabitha (in Greek, Dorcas).[115] If the power was transmitted to Peter, then why not to his successors to this very day? Besides, we have accounts of resurrections not connected with Jesus. Elijah raised a widow's son.[116] Furthermore, non-Christians could also work miracles. Jesus recognized this in the case of miracles of healing. When accused of casting out demons by Beelzebub, he retorted, "If I by Beelzebub cast out demons, how do your sons do it?"[117] He recognized that they did.

The age readily assented to resurrections. We have the case of Appolonius of Tyana who lived in the same century as Jesus. He was an ascetic seer who had traveled to India and on his return was revered as a guru. He was once standing on the edge of a road in Rome when a funeral procession of a young bride was passing by. He halted the mourners. They expected a consoling discourse. Instead he went up to the bier, spoke softly to the girl, told her to arise, and she arose.[118] The account sounds very much like the raising of Jairus' daughter by Jesus.[119] We may gravely doubt whether Christians would credit the miracle of Appolonius, but they certainly belonged to an uncritical age.

The Gospels, however, assure us that they were not uncritical, but rather incredulous on hearing that the Lord was risen. In Luke, we read that, although the disciples had heard of the Lord's appearance to Peter, yet when Jesus came before them they were "startled and frightened and supposed they saw a spirit."[120] And when Thomas was told by the others that they had seen the Lord, he declared that he would not believe unless he could put his hand in the nail prints and the wound.[121] These passages may have been introduced to forestall the insinuation of credulity and we must not so stress it as to deny them any credence.

When we come to the evidences, there are varieties. Shall we stress the empty tomb or the appearances? Was the locale Jerusalem or Galilee? Was the resurrection of a physical or a spiritual body? In Paul's language a terrestrial or a celestial body?

The empty tomb is made the exclusive ground for belief on the part of the disciples by the Jewish scholar Vermes.[122] He points out that the disciples were not expecting the resurrection. Plainly, Jesus had not predicted it. When the news came, they were not disposed to believe and would never have given credence, save for the empty tomb. The argument is not persuasive. When Mary found the tomb empty, her response was, "They have taken away my Lord, and I know not where they have laid him."[123] Had it not been for the appearances, the debate between the Christians and the Jews would have been simply as to who removed the body and why.

There is sufficient evidence that the empty tomb was not decisive for the disciples. The two who encountered the risen Lord at Emmaus had never heard of it. When they reported their experience to the others, the response was, "Yes, he has appeared to Peter."[124] No word of the empty tomb. Paul never refers to it. He tells us that the Lord appeared to five hundred brethren at one time.[125] This must have been in Galilee because immediately following the crucifixion of Jesus as a political pretender 500 of his followers could not have assembled in Jerusalem without provoking arrests. In Galilee there was, of course, no empty tomb, though we cannot be sure that the 500 had no inkling of it.

As for the Jerusalem and the Galilean traditions, there are various combinations. Mark[126] tells us that on the morning after the Sabbath, three women brought spices to the tomb. The stone sealing the tomb had already been removed. A young man in white raiment told them that Jesus was risen. They should tell the disciples and Peter to find him in Galilee. The women fled and told no one, "for they were afraid." Here ends the account in the earliest manuscripts. An odd conclusion indeed! Later manuscripts have added an account of appearances in Jerusalem. The original conclusion centering on Galilee may have been excised, and for it the Jerusalem tradition substituted.

Matthew's gospel centers on Jerusalem.[127] Mary Magdalene and the other Mary came to the tomb. An earthquake rolled away the stone. An angel pointed the women to the empty tomb and informed them that Jesus was risen and had gone to Galilee. They left in great joy to tell the disciples. On the way, Jesus appeared to them and gave instructions to tell the disciples to go to Galilee. This they did.

In Luke's gospel [128] Mary Magdalene and other women from Galilee came to the tomb, which they found empty. Two men in dazzling apparel reminded them that Jesus, while in Galilee, had predicted his death and resurrection. The women reported this to the apostles.

John's gospel, like Matthew's, combines the Galilean and Jerusalem traditions.[129] We learn first that Mary Magdalene alone came to the tomb and, finding it empty, ran to tell Peter and the disciple whom Jesus loved. They confirmed her report. Then Jesus appeared to Mary, who, supposing him to be the gardener, asked where the body of Jesus had been taken. There is no mention of an appearance to Peter and the other disciple. On the same day Jesus appeared to the disciples in the absence of Thomas. We have noted his incredulity. Eight days later, Jesus through a locked door entered the midst of the disciples. Thomas was convinced. Then in the last chapter follow detailed accounts of the appearances in Galilee, the miraculous draft of fishes, the restoration, and the commission to Peter.

A difference as to the nature of the resurrected body appears to divide Luke and John. In Luke, the risen Christ was able to eat a fish.[130] This requires a physical body. In John, the body is so diaphanous as to be able to pass through a closed door.[131] This would require a spiritual body. At the same time in John, Thomas is told to put his finger in Jesus' side. This sounds physical. There are other minor discrepancies. In two versions Peter was the first, in the others, one or more women.

Paul's experience best fits a spiritual resurrection. He counted himself a witness.[132] He may well have had in mind his own conversion, of which there are two accounts in the book of Acts. In Acts 9, he was blinded by a light and heard a voice. His companions heard the voice but saw nothing. In Acts 22, they saw a light but heard nothing. These accounts were not written by Paul but by Luke. Paul says simply that God "called me through his grace," and "was pleased to reveal his Son to me." [133]

There is, however, a very revealing passage in Paul's letter to the Romans where he says that in baptism we were buried with Christ unto death, "so that as Christ was raised from the dead by the glory of the Father, we too might walk in newness of life." [134] This might be taken to mean that resurrection is walking in newness of life. This hint is made more concrete by Athanasius in the fourth century. As evidence of the resurrection he does not appeal to the gospels at all but rather to the power of the risen Christ to bring about newness of life in believers. "Is he a dead Christ who makes the adulterer chaste, the murderer gentle, the scoffer reverent? The barbarians who devoured each other and could not endure for a single moment to be without weapons, having learned of Christ, turn from fighting to husbandry and, instead of arming their hands with weapons, raise them in prayer." [135]

The argument is not, of course, that the resurrection of Jesus was his rising to a new level of life, but that being alive, whatever the nature of the resurrection, he works this transformation in his followers. Testimonies of this sort are continuous.

Similar testimonies are given in our own day. Schweitzer, who looked on Jesus as the great unknown, in response to his call forsook a distinguished career in Europe to take medicine to Africa. A missionary in China during the Japanese occupation relates how, during the persecution of the church, a man in a neighboring town had been beaten by the Japanese police and was in dire need of medical help. No doctor in the city dared go. The missionary called on his own doctor, told him the story without a hint that he should go. He responded, "Of course I'll go. Jesus meant it." John Macmurray suffered a shipwreck of faith in our civilization as a result of the first world war. "As I brooded over this experience I suddenly saw it in the light of what I knew of the life and teaching of Jesus and both were transformed. Jesus himself came alive for me as a real person whom I knew, and what had seemed the meaninglessness of life took on a new meaning." [136] Lincoln Steffens tells of his first encounter with the New Testament. "The experience was an adventure so startling that I wanted everybody else to have it. . . . It is news. . . . Jesus had discovered that he could not save the righteous, only sinners. . . . Christianity, unpreached, untaught, unlearned among the righteous, works wonders still among sinners." [137]

One might say that these witnesses have been affected simply by the reading of the gospels, but they give one the feeling that in some indefinable way a power has laid hold of them.

How crucial, then, is the resurrection? Paul said that without it we are of all men the most miserable.[138] This might mean that if Christ did not rise, we shall not rise. But he argues in reverse with the Corinthians that if we do not rise, he did not rise. Or does he mean that we are the most miserable because Christ does not dwell in us?

The point is sometimes made that without the resurrection there would have been no church, for it has been built on an empty tomb. But Paul found members already in the church at Corinth who did not believe in the resurrection. And what shall we say of the five hundred to whom the Lord appeared in Galilee? There is no proof that they had not heard of the empty tomb, but neither is there any hint that they had. After having assembled in memory of the crucified, if there then had been no appearance, would they have dispersed for good? A resurrection is not essential for the founding of a great religion. What of Manicheeism? What of Islam?

Still there is absolutely no doubt that the resurrection has been cardinal in Christian experience, both as the ground of assurance for our own immortality and as a source of strength and comfort through an indwelling spirit.

The Christ of Faith

If then we turn from the sayings and deeds of Jesus to the proclamation about him in the early church, we are not thereby delivered from the necessity of choices. John Knox has well pointed out [139] that there were three interpretations of Jesus on the part of the early Christian community: gnosticism, kenoticism, and adoptionism. The gnostic view that Jesus was not a genuine human being, but only appeared as if he were, might be inferred from Paul's statement that God sent his Son in the *likeness* of sinful flesh, and again that he was born in the *likeness* of men. But this was certainly not Paul's view, for he said that God sent his Son born of *woman,* and he would certainly have endorsed the statement of the Johannine epistle that it is the spirit of antichrist which denies that Jesus has come in the flesh. Gnosticism, with a considerable following for a time, was definitively rejected.[140]

The word *kenoticism* comes from the Greek term meaning "emptying." The salient verse was the word of Paul that Christ did not "count equality with God a thing to be grasped, but *emptied* himself, taking the form of a servant. Again "though he was rich for our sake he became poor. The verse "He had to be made like his brethren in every respect," might be taken to mean that he divested himself of some divine characteristics. Certainly it was recognized that he divested himself of omniscience, for his saying was recorded that no one knows the hour of the coming of the Son of Man, not even the angels, nor the Son but only the Father and the evidence was given that he was in error when he said that there were those there standing who would not taste of death before seeing the Son of Man come in his kingdom.[141]

The concept of relinquishing equality with God requires a preexistent equality. This is plainly affirmed in Colossians, "He was the first born of all creation and was before all things" (cf. 1:15-19). And this, of course, is the theme of the Johannine prolog. The Logos, God's self-expressive Word, was his agent in creation. This Word became flesh in Christ. There is the further claim that Christ assumed human form in order to redeem humanity. "For God so loved the world that he gave his only Son that whoever believes in him should not perish but have eternal life." He was put to death for our trespasses and raised for our justification.[142]

This called for a plan on the part of God that the death of the Son would atone for the sins of the world. In that case every detail of the drama of redemption must also have been foreordained: that Judas should betray, Peter deny, Annas, Caiaphas and Pilate condemn, and the soldiers drive in the nails. Dante saw the logic and used it to justify the Roman empire as a necessary legal institution because Christ must have been legally convicted of sin in order to pay the legal penalty for sin.[143] What a sorry picture of God is this! How remote from the story of the prodigal son whose father cut short his little speech of contrition, threw his arms around his neck and ordered the robe, the ring, and the fatted calf. The preplanned drama of redemption ill becomes the God who could be called *Abba,* Father.

The foreordination of the crucifixion is declared in John's gospel where Jesus says, "My soul is deeply troubled. Shall I pray, 'Father, save me from this hour?' No, for this purpose I have come to this hour." How foreign is this to the prayer in Gethsemane, "May this cup pass from me." [144]

But although preexistence must be assumed for Paul's picture of the descent of a divine figure, for the concept of self-emptying it is not. The whole earthly ministry of Jesus from the temptation to the cross was precisely that—a rejection of the pursuit of power and glory. [145]

The third view of Christ in the proclamation of the early church is *adoptionism,* that God designated Jesus to be the center of the greatest spiritual crisis in history. A number of texts lend themselves to such an interpretation. "God *made* this Jesus whom you crucified to be both Lord and Christ." Jesus was descended from David according to the flesh and *designated* Son of God in power. Again he was *designated* by God to be a high priest. [146]

When and why did this adoption occur? Some thought at the baptism because Mark's gospel asserts that as Jesus came up from the water a voice from heaven proclaimed, "Thou art my beloved Son." This is a reference to Ps. 2:7. A number of passages point rather to the crucifixion. He was crowned with glory and honor because of the suffering of death. "He became obedient unto death . . . therefore God highly exalted him." For Paul the occasion appears to have been the resurrection. "*Designated* the Son of God by power . . . from the resurrection." [147]

Why was he adopted? In Hebrews, "He learned *obedience* through what he suffered and being made perfect was designated by God as high priest." In Philippians: "*obedient* unto death . . .

and therefore. . . ." And Paul says, "designated . . . according to the spirit of *holiness*." [148] These passages all seem to say that he was adopted because of what he was. This is not an affirmation of a mere human achievement. He was what he was by reason of his relationship to God. But Fuller goes further and suggests that he was what he was by reason of a prior adoption. [149] Designation was foreordination. The above passages suggest rather the contrary. In any case the difficulties inherent in the concept of predestination have already been noted.

One observes that among the reasons assigned for adoption there is no mention of sinlessness, though this might be subsumed under the rubric of "being made perfect." Certainly the early church believed that Jesus was sinless. Paul declared that "for our sake God made him to be sin who was without sin," and in Hebrews, "In every respect he has been tempted even as we are, yet without sin." [150]

The doctrine of the virgin birth may have been devised and certainly has been used to prove that Jesus could have been sinless because he was not contaminated by birth through normal generation which was sullied by the fall of Adam. The Anabaptist Melchior Hofmann went a step further and said that Jesus passed through Mary without contact as through a canal. A papal pronouncement has taken the further step of affirming the immaculate conception of the Virgin Mary. But if she was immaculately conceived, despite the normal process, why not proclaim the immaculate conception of Jesus and drop the virgin birth as superfluous? In any case it is highly dubious on historical grounds. We do not find it in Paul, the earliest writer, nor in Mark, the earliest gospel, nor in John, the Hellenistic gospel. And Matthew's gospel, which does have the doctrine, traces the genealogy of Jesus through Joseph. In Luke's account, which also has the virgin birth, Mary says to the boy Jesus in the temple, "Behold, your *father* and I have been looking for you anxiously." [151]

To form an opinion as to whether Jesus was sinless we do better to look at what he is recorded to have done and said. He was tempted. Some say that temptation itself is sin because it consists in the desire to sin. Luther well disposed of that contention when he said, "You can't stop the birds from flying over your head, but you can keep them from nesting in your hair." [152] Besides, what virtue could there be if one were incapable of sin?

In modern times, Huxley [153] has called into question either the accuracy of the gospel or the integrity of Jesus. In the debate with Gladstone about the miracle of the Gadarene swine, he taxed Jesus with wanton destruction of property. The story is that Jesus expelled from a raving demoniac a legion of demons who begged not to be sent out of the country but be allowed to enter a drove of swine. Jesus consented. Whereupon the animals stampeded over a cliff into the sea and were drowned to the number of 2000. And the swine did not belong to Jesus. Huxley's comment was that either Jesus sinned or he did not perform the miracle. Huxley preferred the second alternative and that took care of that.

An orthodox Jew, we have been told, would regard Jesus' denunciation of the Pharisees as "simply fanatical and outrageous." [154] He might, and he would be mistaken. Jesus was, in a sense, a Pharisee. Over against the Roman occupation, there were three parties. The Sadducees would fraternize, the Zealots rebel. The Pharisees would do neither, but observe the law of the Lord and await his vindication. But what was the law of the Lord? The strict constructionists could debate whether it was lawful to eat an egg laid on the Sabbath.[155] The loose constructions recognized humanitarian considerations.[156] Jesus shared their temper. He did not cut off personal relations, dined three times with a Pharisee and cordially received a "ruler of the Pharisees," named Nicodemus, who later assisted in the deposition of the body from the cross and the entombment. The Pharisees were not consistently alienated from Jesus but sought to save him from Herod.[157]

Yet there was a clash. Jesus objected to their lofty contempt for the herd who ate with unwashed hands. The name Pharisee means "the separated one." Jesus was sent to the lost sheep of the house of Israel and shocked the righteous by eating with tax collectors and harlots. We must further remember that he was a prophet, calling on all alike to repent: Sadducees, Pharisees, Herodians, priests, Levites, scribes, and the very people of Israel who betimes had less faith than Tyre and Sidon.

The most impressive evidence that Jesus himself had feelings of guilt is that he came to be baptized of John whose baptism was for the remission of sins. We have noticed that this presented a problem to the early church. John protested that he might better be baptized by Jesus, and Jesus told him to "fulfill all righteousness." [158] Does this mean that Jesus, standing in no need of repentance, suffered himself for the sake of others, to be baptized as if he did? The natural assumption is that he, too, felt the need. In that case, he is nearer to us and better able to be the "pioneer of our salvation." [159]

His self-consciousness can never be fully fathomed, but we can form some conception of how he conceived of his role by examining his attitude to the titles ascribed to him. Take first the Son of man. A competent Jewish scholar says that in Aramaic, the language of Jesus, this expression could be used for the first person either to avoid a direct statement like our "one would think so," or in self-depreciation like "your humble servant." Never was it a title.[160]

In the sayings of Jesus the expression is frequently a circumlocution for the first person. Jesus says to Judas, "Would you betray the Son of man with a kiss?" And again, "Foxes have holes, and birds of the air have nests; but the Son of man has nowhere to lay his head." Obviously the Son of man is Jesus. There is an instance, however, in which the reference appears to be to someone else. "Whoever is ashamed of me and my words, of him will the Son of man be ashamed." In view of the distinction here made, one need not assume that Jesus was speaking of himself when he said, "There are some standing here who will not taste of death before they see the Son of man coming in his kingdom." [161]

The title, Messiah, presents a difficulty because, after Peter made the confession that Jesus was the Christ (Messiah), Jesus enjoined silence (Matt. 16:20). This may have been a device of the narrator to explain why Jesus never made the claim. But if he did make it, Dodd is quite right that the concept of the Messiah was changed into that of the Suffering Servant.[162] And the same may be said of the title Son of Man who came "not to be ministered unto but to minister." [163]

The title, Son of God, is rare but there is a passage in Matthew's gospel which has the ring of the Johannine discourses. Here Jesus says that "no one knows the Son except the Father, and no one knows the Father except the Son and any to whom the Son chooses to reveal him." [164] Sonship is, then, not exclusive. Jesus is again the pioneer who can lead others into his relationship with the Father.

There is another title, not infrequent in the gospels, of which a learned Jewish scholar rightly complains that Christians have made too little. It is the title, prophet.[165] Jesus says that a prophet is not without honor save in his own country. It is impossible that a prophet should perish outside of Jerusalem. The woman at the well says, "I perceive that you are a prophet." One aghast that Jesus should consort with outcasts comments, "If this man were a prophet. . . ." The Jewish scholar makes much of the texts where the role of Jesus as prophet is connected with Galilee. He is called "Jesus the prophet of Galilee." At the triumphal entry the crowds called out, "This is the prophet Jesus from Nazareth of Galilee." The point is that Galilee was the seat of charismatic prophets and healers of whom two in particular are described.[166]

We end, then, with enigmas, surmizes, and humility before the unfathomable. Whether Jesus thought of himself as more than a rabbi and a prophet we cannot be sure. If he assumed more pretentious roles, it was not to exalt himself but to uplift his people. His concern was with the kingdom of God both present and to come. This is plain, that those who walked with him, talked with him, and ate with him, saw in him no blemish and were brought by him so much closer to God that every symbol, every concept, every title expressive of the interplay of the human and the divine could appropriately be applied to him. On the Hebrew side, Jesus was the Messiah, the Son of man, the Son of God, the Wisdom of God. And on the Hellenistic side, the Reason of the divine indwelling and the divine outgoing as the Word. Rejected of men, he was vindicated by the resurrection, and exalted to the right hand of the throne of God.

Wherein, then, for us does his excellence lie? The Jewish scholar above mentioned speaks of Jesus as "Second to none in profundity of insight and grandeur of character. He is in particular an unsurpassed master of the art of laying bare the inmost core of spiritual truth and of bringing every issue back to the essence of religion, the existential relationship of man to man, and man to God.

"It should be added that in one respect more than any other he differed from both of his contemporaries and even his prophetic predecessors. The prophets spoke on behalf of the honest poor, and defended the widows and the fatherless, those oppressed and exploited by the wicked, rich and powerful. Jesus went further. In addition to proclaiming them blessed, he actually took his stand among the pariahs of his world, those despised by the respectable. Sinners were his table-companions and the ostracized tax-collectors and prostitutes his friends." [167]

The excellency of Jesus came for Paul Tillich, who in the thirties had considered his existence unimportant to consist in the fifties in this that he became the Christ because he effaced himself as the actual person of history.[168] Tillich saw the effacement in the myth of the descent of a divine figure who came down to earth to share our lot. I would stress rather the concrete leader of a little band who with a towel over his arm sank to his knees before a basin of water and in the role of a slave washed the grime from the feet of peasants.

Nor are self-effacement and humility adequate concepts since they have a touch of the negative. More important are the positive qualities of compassion, tenderness, and the absence of rancor, so that even when nailed to the cross Jesus could cry, "Father, forgive." Where in all history before him is there anything comparable? The historical critic may suggest that the words were placed in his mouth. Very well, but what sort of a person must he have been into whose mouth such words could fittingly be placed? Here is an excellence beyond our comprehension. We can but in amazement, awe, and gratitude fall to our knees.

What does all this have to say as to our humanity? Jesus was human. The church has never denied his humanity, his full humanity. If then a human being actually exhibited such excellence, if Jesus was not a literary figment of the general human aspiration but an actual exemplification of astounding goodness, this does say something about the potentialities of humankind. It invests with meaning the translation of the opening verses of the Epistle to the Hebrews in the Revised Standard Version that he is the *pioneer* of our faith. Now a pioneer is someone who does something for the first time which others can do after him. Columbus was a pioneer in the sense that he first opened up the new world to the old. No one else can ever be the first, but millions have since traversed the ocean. Lindbergh was the first to fly across the Atlantic. No one else can be first. Millions have followed. Even so Jesus opened for us new heights of human achievement. With God's help, indeed, but this also is available to us. What he was we can become. He is our pioneer.

And what does he tell us about God? Some say we cannot reason from man to God. Revelation must come down from above. But how are we to know that it is revelation? How can we arrive at God whom we have not seen unless we begin with man whom we have seen? Can we not move from the created to the Creator? To be sure whatever we venture to say will be pitifully inadequate, but not on that account false.

Harriet Beecher Stowe well framed the leap from man in Christ to God in her story of a boy, Jim, lost at sea and not converted.[169] The mother was crazed believing that the unconverted were irretrievably lost. The black mammy, Candace, took her on her lap and rocked her as a babe. " 'Honey, darlin', ye ain't right,— dar's a dreadful mistake somewhar,' she said, 'Why, de Lord ain't like what ye tink,—He loves ye, honey! Why, jes' feel how I loves ye,—poor ole black Candace,—an' I ain't better 'n Him as made me!' "

That's it. "I ain't better 'n Him as made me!" We can approach God through the analogies, however, inadequate, of man. We can use the words formulated in John's gospel in the mouth of Jesus, "He who has seen me has seen the Father." We have here seen God as compassion, justice and mercy, forgiveness, succor in our infirmities, power in weakness and the magnet who draws us to himself.

The Church
and History

The church and history has two aspects: the Christian concept of history and the role of the church in history. They are closely related. With respect to the first, Christianity emerged from Judaism. The Christians, like the Jews, believed that God created the world and found it good. He created man in his own image. Among men, he chose a particular people whom he delivered from bondage in Egypt, to whom he gave a land and with whom he made a covenant that he would be their God and they should be his people. Ogden Nash quipped, "How odd of God to choose the Jews!" His cleverness was profound. How odd indeed that a tiny people overshadowed by the land of the pyramids and the hanging gardens of Babylon should have survived after all the empires of antiquity are as Nineveh and Tyre, and that this pawn of the powers should have exerted a greater influence than any other on the beliefs and institutions of the western world.

The salient word in the Jewish concept of history was God.[170] He it was who raised up and cast down. He had given to his people the law, the Torah, that they should keep his commandments, but they were a stiffnecked generation who time and again rebelled. Disasters were their chastisements. Many succumbed but always a remnant survived. Disasters which fell upon the innocent could no longer be regarded as chastisements. One explanation was that they would not last long and the earth would again blossom as Eden. Another was that the sufferings of the chosen would be for the healing of the nations.

These concepts were the heritage of Christianity. One might have thought that they would have lost all meaning because in Christ all things had become new. History in the old sense was at an end. Nevertheless, the link with the past was not severed. The church was not merely the successor to Israel. It was Israel,[171] the new Israel of God, the chosen people, the elect nation. Christians were the sons of Abraham, circumcized not in the flesh but in the spirit. As the Psalmist looked forward to the day when all nations would go up to Mount Zion to receive the word of the Lord, so now all peoples, the Jews included, would be embraced in the new Jerusalem coming down out of heaven.

The links with the past consisted of prophecy and typology. Matthew frequently says that something happened that the word of the prophet might be fulfilled.[172] That was why Jesus was born of a virgin, in the city of Bethlehem, in the seed of David and went down into Egypt. Typology did not involve the cyclical view of history but that certain themes were recurrent till they found their fulfillment in Christ. Moses, lifting up the serpent in the wilderness, was the type of Christ lifted up on the cross. The passage through the Red Sea was the type of baptism. The sacrifice of Isaac prefigured both salvation by faith and the performance of good works.[173]

There was little periodizing of the Old Testament by the early Christians. They noted, of course, the dispensations of Adam, Noah, Abraham, and Moses. But after Moses, the line for Paul ran straight to Christ. The purpose of the law was to show man his inability to keep it, that humbled he might trust to salvation through Christ. Jesus himself said that he had come to fulfill both the law and the prophets without differentiation.

Such was the background of early Christian thought. The church was the new Israel of God. What then was her role in history? The answer was simple. There would be no more history after the manner of the Old Testament. The Son of man would come to preside over the great assize. But he did not come. What then? Two answers. Be patient. A day in God's sight is as a thousand years. He is delaying to give further opportunity for repentance.[174] This answer did not long satisfy, and there followed successive setting of dates even to our own day.

Another answer was that the delay really did not matter. Years are not significant, only life, eternal life, not just going on forever, but a new quality of living in the spirit. There is a leap from time into the timeless. This it is to be born again, not in the flesh but in the spirit. Such was the Johannine picture.

This did not answer the question of what to do during the interval of waiting. The Christian, if continuing to exist, had still to eat, drink, work, and sleep and, what's more, live with non-Christian neighbors. Now came the problem of the church in history. What of the relation of the church to the world during the interim?

In the centuries up to Constantine, there were three answers. One was segregation. "Come out of her, my people."[175] The rigorist sects made the attempt: the Montanists, Marcionites, and Novationists, and the monastic movement is claimed to have had its beginnings among the latter. At the end of the first century the author of Revelation could cry, "Fallen, fallen is Babylon the great," meaning Rome. In the third century Commodianus could welcome a Gothic invasion to overthrow the empire drunk with the blood of the saints. At the other pole were those who appreciated the empire because the *Pax Romana* had opened the seas and the roads for the dissemination of the gospel. This was the attitude of several of the bishops of Asia Minor.[176]

The prevalent view lay in between. Paul could describe the deified emperor as "the son of perdition whom the Lord Jesus would slay with the breath of his mouth." At the same time there is a power which restrains chaos and this appears to be the empire. Paul recognized that the non-Christian world was not wholly bad. The Jews had the Torah and the Gentiles the law of nature. Paul was proud of his Roman citizenship and did not disdain to appeal to Caesar. Government was ordained of God to punish the bad and protect the good, though the government at that time was not Christian.[177]

At the same time Paul excoriated Gentile vices. The evangelist Luke alone among the New Testament writers took cognizance of secular history. Christ was born when a decree went out from Augustus Caesar and Quirinius was governor of Syria. John the Baptist made his appearance in the fifteenth year of Tiberius and all the minor rulers, Gentile and Jewish, are named. In the book of Acts we have reference to Festus, Felix, and Agrippa, and since the book was written prior to the martyrdoms of Peter and Paul, the Roman government could be regarded as the protector of the Christians against the Jews.

At the same time there were so many areas of dissociation that Christians were accused of hatred of the human race. On two counts they held aloof: religion and morals.[178] The Christians would not worship the pagan gods and above all else would not put a pinch of incense on the altar of the deified emperor. This, in the eyes of the government, was their major offense and the ground of persecution. A religious culture provides more areas of conflict over religion than a secular. The schools involved religion because Homer and Virgil were taught not simply as classics but as textbooks of religion. Even the hospitals presented a problem because they were under the aegis of Asclepius, the god of healing. On the moral side, gladiatorial combats were taboo and so also the theatre because the plays were lewd. The courts of law were eschewed because Christians should not turn to pagans to settle disputes. Let them go to the bishops. And a Christian could not be a judge with authority to enact the penalty of death. The church abhorred the shedding of blood. One church order allowed a Christian to be in the army only in case he did not kill.

The conversion of Constantine and his public espousal of Christianity brought a great change in Christian thinking and deportment.[179] (He became emperor of both East and West in A.D. 324.) For twenty years in civil wars he had been seeking to protect the Christians and when at last victorious, he was hailed as the Lord's anointed. His own view was that with the sword he had overcome the warring states inspired by demons and now he trusted that Christianity would dispel the demons and usher in universal peace. How grievously was he to be disappointed when Christians quarreled to the blood!

Yet Christian divisions did not becloud an optimistic picture of the relations of church and state. Constantine's adviser, Bishop Eusebius of Caesarea could regard the empire and the church as joint works of God for the saving of the world. At the same point in history, the empire had been established under Augustus and Christianity inaugurated by the birth of Christ. Unhappily the two had long been at odds but now happily they were united to fulfill their role in setting up a Christian world order with one God, one Lord, one faith, one baptism, and one Constantine. The church was then drawn into the sphere of public affairs and her juridical rulings were given the force of law. Bishops, such as Eusebius in the East and Hosius in the West, became advisers to the emperor.

A century later came the barbarian invasions in the West, attributed by the still surviving pagans to the displeasure of the gods over the spread of Christianity. Augustine replied by pointing to all the calamities which befell Rome before Christianity was on the scene. He then went on to elaborate a philosophy of history devoid of romanticism about the empire. "What are great states without justice," he asked, "if not robbery on a grand scale?" From Horace he picked up the theme of the virus of corruption in the Roman blood, and from Sallust the excoriation of the destruction of Carthage. Augustine himself was a north African and his pages reverberate with the curses of the conquered. Reminded of the Roman peace, "Yes," he retorted, "and achieved by how much shedding of blood!" Still he recognized that Rome had certain virtues and there had been improvement starting not with Augustus but with the conversion of emperors such as Constantine and Theodosius. There is a hint here of the possibility of progress.

And then he says, "The Church now begins her reign." Just what does that mean? Is it an intimation of theocracy? Or is it just a spiritual reign. He certainly did not regard the total church as the new Israel of God. It was composed of wheat and weeds. So too, of course, was the state. He does not talk about church and state but about the cities or commonwealths of the world and of God. The dualism is not between institutions but between the invisible companies of the lost and the redeemed, who are pilgrims and strangers traveling to a consummation beyond history. Still they are not to be indifferent to what is going on. The empire, for all its faults, represents the principle of order and should be defended by force of arms against the barbarians.

The ambiguities made it possible for nearly every party in the later ages to appeal to him.[180]

After him three main types emerge with respect to the role of the church in history and naturally as to the theory of history. The church can dominate society, withdraw from society, or collaborate with society.[181]

The concept of domination was obviously not possible in the age of persecution. And neither Constantine nor Theodosius, nor Justinian, despite ecclesiastical legislation, contemplated setting up a theocracy. For that we turn to the Gregorian reform from the eleventh through the thirteenth centuries. In the fifteenth we have the Florence of Savonarola; in the sixteenth of Calvin at Geneva and the ultra Calvinists in Holland, of Knox and the General Assembly in Scotland; in the seventeenth of Cromwell's Ironsides and of the Holy Commonwealths of New England. They all depended on coercion of which too much is self-defeating. If the body ruled does not subscribe to the faith of the theocrats they are doomed.

Another way is withdrawal. We find it in monasticism and sectarianism. In the period of Constantine there was a great wave of monasticism. Harnack said that when the masses entered the church the elite went to the desert. In the West, monasticism was at first withdrawn from society. The Benedictine houses were erected on inaccessible islands or mountains. But when the gospel crossed the Alps, the monasteries became centers for the conversion of the countryside. The Cluniacs became entertainers par excellence. The Cistercians revived the rigor of earlier rule, but then became prosperous wool growers and waxed cold.[182] The Friars instituted a new type of monasticism—in the world but not of the world. They had no fixed abodes, went into the fields and cities as preachers and into the universities as teachers.

The Church and History

Sectarianism involved a separation from the world and also from the church. The monastics were always in danger of sectarianism if the popes were not wise enough to endorse their programs. In the late Middle Ages we have a pullulation of sects. The best known are the Waldensees and the Hussites which still survive. The Lollards in England fed into the Reformation. The Reformation itself, from the point of view of Rome, was itself sectarian, but the main varieties, the Calvinist, Lutheran, Anglican, and Zwinglian did not repudiate affiliation with the state. The more radical reformers, notably the Anabaptists, established isolated enclaves on the estates of noblemen who would tolerate their pacifism because they were good farmers. Their initial intent was not isolation because they hoped to convert the whole society. They have survived either through persecution from without or deliberate isolation from within. If they fraternize with the world they soon become of the world. The Amish in Indiana are in danger because, unable to buy more land to sustain their expanding offspring, the young men are permitted to work in factories. That may be the beginning of the end.

The third approach is one of affiliation, or partnership. In the early Middle Ages, the Holy Catholic Church and the Holy Roman Empire could think of themselves as the correlative branches of a Christian society. We have noticed how this balance was upset by the theocratic Gregorian reform which reached the point of claiming under Innocent IV that the sacerdotal authority, alone able to confer salvation, had also authority to delegate jurisdiction to the secular rulers. Luther undercut the theory by his assertion of the priesthood of all believers, including the civil rulers. He returned basically to the early medieval pattern of partnership with a vocational division. The church and the state represent the religious and the civil branches of the culture. The state deals with the earthly, the church with the heavenly. The state handles crime, the church sin. Every crime is a sin, but not every sin is a crime. Princes rule castles, churchmen formulate creeds. The state uses the sword, the church the word. There were not two ethics. Both were motivated by love, but rather two codes of behavior.

There is another variety of vocationalism which is not quite so much of a partnership. The state and the church have the same objectives with divergent means. But neither side approves of the means used by the other. We have an example in the case of Origen in the early church. He held that Christians should not go to war. Celsus told him that if all in the empire were of that mind the barbarians would take over. Origen replied that if the empire were so Christian as not to fight, the missionary zeal of the Christians would have converted the barbarians and restrained them. But Origen conceded that if the empire engaged in a just war, Christians would pray for its success through declining to participate. Neither side wanted a barbarian invasion. The Christian could not condone war, but could see a difference between wars, and could pray that the just war would succeed rather than the unjust.

A similar dichotomy was voiced by the Quaker, Elton Trueblood, who said that he could not find it in his heart to criticize England for going to war against Hitler.[183] Quakers, too, abhorred tyranny, but would seek to overcome it not by arms but by the renunciation of arms and by acts of mercy. And after a war, reconciliation could the more readily be achieved through those who had had no part in the carnage. This stance he called "vocational Christian pacifism."

This suggests a modification of Reinhold Niebuhr's *Moral Man and Immoral Society*.[184] The title is catchy, but something of a misnomer, as Niebuhr recognized, for moral man is a constituent of immoral society. His point was that the same individual may behave morally in private relations but immorally in the cut-throat competitions of commerce and politics. But to call society immoral will not do, unless one specifies what sort of a society. Niebuhr undoubtedly had in mind the entire populace of a country. He was perfectly right that such an unweeded group cannot be counted on to measure up to Christian standards. A society consisting of all the inhabitants of an area may be capable of magnanimity, but not of sacrifice. There are, however, societies capable of just that. The Quakers call themselves the *Society* of Friends, a society with a selected constituency, whose members belong not by reason of birth and infant baptism, but through commitment to an ideal. In other words, the monastic orders and the sects, such as the Quakers, are societies and are capable of being moral.

But their members can never expect to be the rulers of an un-weeded society without a measure of compromise. Sigismund Stary, king of Poland, said "I am the king of sheep and goats." And if he went too far in overriding the goats they would butt him out of his kingship. This does not mean that a Christian in executive office should go contrary to his conscience. If that is required, he should resign. But he cannot expect to achieve all of his ideals. A Christian in a legislative body, however, in par-liament or Congress, can agitate for the undiluted ideal, at least more readily. The constituency still has to be considered. But it is easier to persuade a small state than an entire nation. We have seen men like Borah and LaFollette who were able for long to stay in office, though voicing opinions not generally popular. Again, the head of a minority party may engage in a political campaign with no hope of victory but as a device for educating the public. One thinks of Norman Thomas. In some instances the ruler and the prophet have recognized each other. Franklin D. Roosevelt is said to have confessed a debt to Norman Thomas, and Reinhold Niebuhr recognized that even the fanatic may be of some use.

I am saving for the next section an example of complete unanimity as to the objectives with divergent strategies supportive of each other.

Today and
What Next?

The title of this book, *Yesterday, Today and What Next?* suggests an equal treatment of all three, but the allotment for the past far exceeds that for the other two. One reason is that the extent of the past is much greater and the knowledge of it much less than for the present about which we are all at least moderately informed. As for the future what we now strive to achieve may determine what is to be. Lest in our forecasts we bog down in the slough of despond or soar in the clouds of fantasies, we do well to assess the possibilities in the light of what has been and now is.

Where, then, are we? We are in the third great convulsion of history in the West. The first was the period when B.C. became A.D., the age of Augustus and of Christ. The Western world was then at peace by reason of the Roman conquests. The victories brought in multitudes of the enslaved. They were more profitably employed on vast Italian estates from which the small farmers were dislodged. These flocked to Rome to the number of some 200,000, kept from restlessness by the dole of bread and circuses. Ease of travel made possible an influx of oriental peoples and religions, often organistic cults. The old gods were dying, the sturdy virtues of rural Rome eroded. Tacitus could say of Rome that it was where "all things base and abominable flow together and are celebrated." [185] And out of this welter arose Christianity.

The second great crisis was that of the sixteenth century of which Erasmus said, "This is the worst century since Jesus Christ." [186] The vase of the medieval synthesis was already cracked when the Reformation shattered the fragments. Revolution, wars of religion, the revival of the Inquisition, and epidemics of witchcraft followed. Out of this turmoil emerged a new dynamism marked by capitalism, democracy, religious liberty, and an amazing advance in technology.

Survivals and advance through these crises suggest hope. But in many ways our rifts are deeper and our perils more ominous. The cleavage between Protestantism and Catholicism was within the Christian frame. Now we have Fascism and Communism, which drop God and yet carry over from the religious tradition a fervent dynamism, intolerance, and apocalypticism, with readiness to liquidate even millions of individuals in the present in order to realize a more equitable and enriching culture in the future. The West is basically conservative, but at the same time fluctuating, confused, bewildered, consumed at times with rage and scorn, subject to psychic collapse, seeking release sometimes by flight into the ethereal, sometimes in ecstatic shrieks of defiant jubilation. The ancient values are questioned, scrutinized, rejected. With reason do we ask "What's next?"

Our situation is in part an illustration of the failures of success in the sense of the undesirable concomitants of the goal achieved. Technology in this era has made greater advance in decades than ever before in centuries. We have prolonged life at both ends by reducing infant mortality and extending old age. The concomitant of the increase in population is the threat of starvation. Technology provides, however, a corrective through contraception and sterilization. But then comes another unforeseen concomitant. It is one thing to make a discovery, another to get it used. The most prolific peoples today are those emotionally unready to avail themselves of the resources.

Technology has relieved us of drudgery. We need not bestir ourselves to get out of bed to shut off or turn on the television. At the same time, the work that must be done to sustain the technology is reduced to boredom by mechanization. What more deadly than the endless insertion of pins into slots! This boredom is not, however, wholly due to the introduction of the machine as such but rather is the result of mass production which is possible even in the case of handicrafts. In Berne I once saw a carver turning out little wooden bears, all day long, year in, year out, bears, bears, bears. Every stroke of his knife must have become automatic. But at any rate he could see at nightfall completed bears and that is more than can be said of the fabrication of an automobile.

However boring work may be, the lack of it is worse. The machine displaces the laborer and increases unemployment. Resistance against it began in the eighteenth century with the smashing of the looms in the Ludlow riots. Another way to escape the machine is simply not to use it. In Mexico, when a team of Quakers was assisting road building by bringing in truckloads of gravel the natives objected: "The creek has pebbles. We have children. Why not give them something to do, carrying handfuls?" Again in India I heard of a project to build a huge dam. The question was whether to use machinery or hand labor. The cost would be equal. The hand labor would take two years longer. The vote was for hand labor.

The most serious concomitant of the success of technology is the exhaustion of energy. Some years ago, when we were blithely unconcerned, a scientist told me he would give us a hundred years with gasoline, a thousand with nuclear power. We have since shortened the span. The situation is not hopeless. There will be heat from the sun and the bowels of the earth for many a day, and power from the wind, the myriad waterfalls, and endless tides. Yet apparently this planet cannot support life indefinitely and exhaustion of energy hastens the end.

Technology has enabled us to reach the limits of geographical expansion. By reason of these advances, the Americas have been able to accommodate huge populations who could not so readily have subdued the wilderness with the more primitive methods. During the nineteenth century, the European pressures were relieved by the open Americas. The underprivileged, restless elements flocked to these shores. This was a major factor in the diminution of wars. From 1800 to 1900 there were no major conflicts. The safety valve is now shut off. The frontier is gone. The conflicts of the future cannot be settled by migration. Witness the difficulties of Israel in finding a homeland.

This brings us to the most fearful concomitant of technology which threatens the existence of the very goal itself. If the earth is rendered uninhabitable by the advanced weaponry, there'll be no more technology.

What can we do about it? Some say socialism, because capitalism inevitably breeds wars, whereas socialism need not. A recent work replies that there would be little difference, because both are seeking to develop technology. This requires energy. No state at this point is self-sufficient. There must be an importation. Payment will have to come from the income of sales abroad. Then will ensue conflicts over markets, issuing in wars.[187]

The solution most commonly proposed is the balance of power. It has occasionally in the past limited war particularly in the case of a congeries of states fairly equal in power, with a common culture and no desire to exterminate each other. This was true of the Greek city-states and they did settle many disputes by arbitration. Nevertheless they devoured each other until taken over by Macedon and Rome. The Italian city-states in the fifteenth century afford another example. Florence, Milan, Venice, Naples and Rome reduced war largely to summer skirmishes. At the end of the season the prisoners were exchanged and the chips counted. Still, Italy was racked by conflicts until swept by the French incursion into the maelstrom of European rivalries. In the eighteenth century the European states were similarly situated. Wars were relatively humane because soldiers were paid and not tempted to pillage. Commanders of mercenaries, loath to lose their men, tried to wear out opponents by endless maneuvers. But battles when they came were bloody, and the end of the century was marked by the French revolution and the rise of Napoleon.

The basic reason why the balance of power has never worked is that it has never been intended by the participants as a genuine balance. Each side has striven to unbalance the balance in its own favor. If one state succeeded in overtopping the rest, the weaker promptly gained preponderant strength by coalition. The Emperor Charles V, in the sixteenth century, spent his entire career in the balancing act. If he crushed France she was speedily succored by Venice, Rome, the Turks, and England. And when his troops sacked Rome, another coalition confronted him.

If the intent were genuinely for a balance, each power should share all of its military secrets with the rest. That was the theory which led Claus Fuchs to transmit atomic secrets to the Russians. If guilty, Fuchs should not have been imprisoned nor the Rosenbergs executed, but rather commended for contributing to the balance.

The theory of the balance requires that no state should make permanent friends of others, only temporary allies. During the second world war I heard a political scientist counsel us Americans not to defeat Germany and Japan too badly. We might need Germany against Russia, and Japan against China. And that was why after the war we were more ready to restore our defeated foes than to aid our victorious allies. The English had reason to complain that the Marshall plan did more for Germany, Italy, and Japan than for England.

This balance of power situation differs today from that in the past. A modern observer points out that one cannot balance a two-legged stool.[188] There must be at least three legs. The Greeks, the Italians, and the more recent European states numbered from four to half a dozen. We have only the United States and Russia. The day may come when there will be four, according to continents: Europe, Asia, Africa, and the Americas. But that day is not yet. A further point is that the previous examples were united as to culture and largely as to language and religion. Today Russia and the United States are divided as to language, economic structure, communism vs. capitalism, and religion (atheism vs. a Judaeo-Christian tradition).

What then is left? Some say the balance of terror. It differs from the old balance of power because the atomic bomb may confer power on the weakest. If Albania were to get the bomb she might highjack Russia. This is why the great powers discourage proliferation. But there is no assurance that one of them may not see fit so to arm a satellite. In any case the balance of terror is very precarious. Modern wars will not be fought with bayonets but with buttons, push-buttons. What if an operator pushes the wrong one? Atrocities may be diminished because there will be no heat of battle to occasion a Mylai massacre, but destruction will be incalculably increased because the expert at the switchboard will not be repelled by actually seeing the devastation wrought.

Today and What Next?

Some justify the balance of terror on the ground that our side would never inflict it. We would have the bomb so as to deter the potential enemy but we would never use it. That is bluffing and a bluff is likely to be called. Whether we would use it or not, the expense of maintaining it is devastating. The great powers devote the largest item in their budgets to military expenditure. We are exhausting our supplies of energy, debasing the currency, wiping out accumulated wealth by inflation, and bringing the world to the brink of bankruptcy.

The possibilities becloud our spirits, and may well be a major cause of the increase in psychic disorders. A grandson wrote me, "Grandpa, the difference between you and me is that when you were my age you thought you'd live to grow up."

"Yes, but what is the alternative?" we are asked. "Is it not the choice between security based on mutual fear or else submission to tyranny?" Would the tyranny be so frightful as to warrant the readiness to inflict or even threaten to inflict death on one or two million people? There are indeed curtailments of liberty in communist satellites which those of our ilk would find exceedingly galling. But there are vast numbers who would not vent their feelings in the perfervid oratory of Patrick Henry's "Give me liberty or give me death." In 1948 a friend of mine, living close to the East German border, told me that he had enough money to buy a car to flee if the Russians advanced, or to buy a house. He bought the house. During the summer of 1975 I was in Poland on an academic mission. I discovered that there are Poles who go abroad, earn more than they could at home, and then, despite all the restrictions, return to spend it. Those whose chief concern is for work, food, and shelter will leave it to intellectuals to envy unmuzzled dogs.

I am not for a moment suggesting that those who advocate maintaining the balance of terror are not inwardly torn asunder.

Today and What Next?

I heard that Reinhold Niebuhr had said were there to be a Russian attack on the United States he would hope to be killed in the assault, thus to be spared the onus of retaliation. I can well believe him to have said it. His mood was that of the judge described by St. Augustine, who would mount the bench to administer justice, while praying, "O God, deliver me from my necessities."

Anyone who can say that, has passed from the pragmatic and prudential into the realm of the moral. We are led then to examine the Christian ethic of war as formulated throughout the centuries.

There has not been a single Christian ethic, but instead three: pacifism, the just war and the crusade.[189] Each has antecedents in Hebrew and classical antiquity. Pacifism in the Old Testament could mean nonresistance and trust for vindication at the hands of the Lord. Rely not on the smoking firebrands of Assyria and Babylon. Trust not to the chariots and horses of Egypt. "In quietness and confidence shall be your strength." Again there was the peace of prudence. Rebellion for the exiles would be futile. Let them accept the peace of Babylon. And there was a redemptive pacifism. The servant of the Lord by his suffering "should bring forth judgment for the gentiles and by his stripes we are healed." On the Greek side, we find lamentations over the brutality, the irrationality and the costliness of war, though no examples of actual refusal to fight, unless one thinks of the cynic who eliminated the possibility of being attacked by having nothing of which he could be despoiled.

On the Christian side, until the time of Constantine, no Christian author condoned killing in war. There was great aversion to the shedding of blood whether in war or in the administration of civil justice. Pacifism had different slants. Tertullian was legalistic. Jesus told Peter to put up his sword and thereby disarmed every soldier. Vindication of the oppressed would speedily come through the return of the Lord. Origen was optimistic that all the world would be Christianized and the barbarians would no longer be a menace. But there were some Christians in the army and the Canons of Hippolytus allowed their presence provided they did not kill. One could be in the Roman army for a lifetime without ever being called upon to kill. The army had many functions which we might call public works.

A century after Constantine, Martin of Tours remained in the army until a battle was imminent, and then he refused to kill. Luckily for him the enemy withdrew. Between the Canons of Hippolytus and Martin, the Council of Arles (A.D. 314) decreed that a Christian should be excommunicated who laid down his arms *in peacetime*. This left open the possibility that he might *in wartime*. But when Constantine was converted in the course of a battle, and for twenty years engaged in wars in part to liberate Christians, his victory was met with a peal of jubilation in which critique of the method was muted.

The concept of the just war originated with the Greeks. Plato said that the object of war must be the vindication of justice and the restoration of peace, never the extermination or enslavement of the conquered. The land should not be ravaged and violence should not be indiscriminate, for among the enemy many are innocent. Cicero elaborated further. War must be conducted only under the authority of the state. Revolution means anarchy. Wars must be openly declared and peace aims laid down at the outset. Good faith must be kept with the enemy. The distinction between the innocent and the guilty on the enemy side is recognized but there is no explicit declaration that noncombatants are to be spared.

Augustine wove together the strands from the classical and Christian views. The private citizen must suffer injury without resistance. Only the state may engage in armed defense. The object of the war must be, as with Plato and Cicero, the vindication of justice and the restoration of peace, with the addition that the motive must be love. This is possible because love is not an act but a disposition. A war can be just on one side only. A just war requires an unjust war, though the rules for the conduct of the war can be observed by both sides. The justice of the war is to be determined by the ruler, since the soldier is not in a position to know. He must give obedient service even to a pagan emperor, such as Julian the Apostate. There is only an implicit exemption of noncombatants from attack but an explicit exclusion of the clergy and the monks from service. The clergy must have bloodless hands to administer the Eucharist, and the monks have forsaken the world.

During the next eight centuries of repeated foreign incursions in the west the rules were grievously attenuated. With the recovery in the eleventh century of a relative stability, an attempt was made to curb warfare. The Truce of God forbad warring on holy days of which there were so many as to reduce war to an occasional diversion. The Peace of God specifically enumerated a list of noncombatants to be exempt from attack. The oath taken by Robert the Pious (996-1031) reads:

> I will not infringe on the church in any way. I will not hurt a cleric or a monk if unarmed. I will not steal an ox, cow, pig, sheep, goat, ass, or a mare with colt. I will not attack a villein or villeiness or servants or merchants for ransom. I will not take a mule or a horse, male or female, or a colt in pasture from any man from the calends of March to the feast of All Saints unless to recover a debt. I will not burn houses or destroy them unless there is a knight inside. I will not root up vines. I will

not attack noble ladies travelling without husband nor their maids, nor widows or nuns unless it is their fault. From the beginning of Lent to the end of Easter I will not attack an unarmed knight.

The late Middle Ages and the Renaissance introduced the principle of proportionate damage. A war would be immoral if the predictable damage would exceed the predictable gain. The recognition that a war could not be just on both sides came when the American Indians in their invincible ignorance justly resisted the just right of the Spaniards to travel in their domains.

Along with the great peace campaign of the eleventh century emerged the crusade. The concept of the holy war has marked Judaism and her two daughters Christianity and Islam because all three believe in only one God who demands obedience from his followers and will visit upon them his displeasure if they go awhoring after false gods. In the Old Testament, Israel was to smite the Hivites, Jebusites, Amalekites, Moabites, and Philistines. In the year 1095 at the Council of Claremont, Pope Urban II made a great peace speech, calling upon the leaders of the Franks to put from them all hatred, all quarrels, all wars, and unite to "deliver the Holy Sepulchre of our Lord polluted by the filthiness of an unclean nation." And all the assembly cried *Deus vult,* "God wills it." Peace at home was to be fostered by a war abroad and the peace campaign turned into a crusade.

The theologians did not recognize the crusade as different from the just war. What could be more just than a holy war? But there were differences. The authority of the state was not necessary. A crusade could be conducted not by a king but by an inspired leader. The knight did not enlist at the behest of the state. He took the cross voluntarily. The object of the war was not the vindication of justice as to land and goods, but the attempt to defend or implement an idea. And the restraints of the code of the just war were readily lifted when the enemy was God's enemy. Cromwell put it well when he said that the soldier "must love his enemies as they are his enemies and hate them as they are God's enemies." Crusades have frequently been marked by atrocities. None can be so inhumane as the champions of a righteous cause.

How much have we left now of these former concepts? As for pacifism we have small minorities who call for nonresistance or nonviolent resistance. Augustine's stipulation that the motives must be love is not wholly unrealistic. There are gentlemen in war devoid of personal resentment, but wars have never been won without enlisting the rabble, and a populace cannot be lashed into a fury without invoking the furies. The crusading mood was prevalent in the United States in the first world war to make the world safe for democracy and to end all war. The second world war was fought in the spirit of the mournful warrior resolved to discharge a repulsive duty. The Communist states have not relinquished their crusading ardor.

The just war's exclusion of revolution broke down during the religious strife of the age of the Reformation. When the Emperor Charles V was minded to come to Germany to stamp out Lutheranism, the inevitable question was whether he could be legitimately resisted. The jurists pointed out that the state has several layers of rulers. The lower might resist the higher. This meant in Germany the electors against the emperor; in France, the princes of the blood against the crown; in England, parliament against the king. When then the democratic idea took hold that the people constitute the state, war became a matter of a state against a state and could thus be fought under the authority of the state.

The stipulation that war must be declared was violated by

Germany's invasion of Belgium and by Pearl Harbor. Keeping good faith with the enemy has not been too scrupulously observed. In some countries the clergy and the monks are not exempt from military service and the church has acquiesced.

The most serious and irreversible erosion is at the point of sparing noncombatants. We even find a justification for killing the innocents. I recall that when Mussolini invaded Ethiopia, a speaker advocated armed intervention to stop him. I asked, "Would you bomb Rome and kill women and children?" "Why not?" came the reply, "Is life any more sacred because it is young?" I would answer, "Not more sacred, but less responsible." As a matter of fact the sparing of noncombatants has never been a complete possibility. In a beleaguered city the weaker, the children, the aged, and the sick would be the first to die of hunger. In 1948, I visited Germany when the effects of the food blockage were still visible and the bones of the aged so protruded that sitting down was painful.

The great turning point which completely obliterated the distinction of combatant and noncombatant was the introduction of obliteration bombing at Guernica, Dresden, Rotterdam, Rheims, and Coventry. And all of this was prior to the use of the atomic bomb on Hiroshima and Nagasaki. Today nuclear war is against entire populations. The more war improves in technology the more it declines in morality. Paul Ramsey well says that the Christian can never acquiesce in the slaughter of noncombatants. He would attack a purely military area such as a navy at sea where all aboard would be combatants. But wars are not won simply by knocking out navies. Since Ramsey would exclude all indiscriminate warfare and since no war can be won without it, for practical purposes under modern conditions he has become a pacifist.[190]

The only Christian course appears to me to be unilateral disarmament. Admittedly this would be no light undertaking. Factories would have to be retooled and workers retrained and otherwise employed. Lasting change calls for vast changes in our social structure. Years ago Horace Taft, the brother of the president, said to me with respect to our ills, "I see no solution which is not radical." (That is to say, drastic.) A recent analyst of the problem of disarmament concludes that the difficulties are not insuperable.[191]

If the United States were to disarm unilaterally, what would be the effect? How would the Russians react? I suspect at first with incredulity. We would have to convince them that this was no ruse by dismantling bases abroad and munition factories at home. If convinced of our good faith, they might follow suit. I realize that at this juncture our nation could not be induced to take so drastic a step, but even a minor reduction might well bring reciprocity if obviously prompted not by weakness but by good will. But if not, if the Russians were to take over, what then? I do not think they would. Operating this country with an obstructionist populace would be an impossible task, especially in view of the distance. The oceans do for us what the channel long did for England.

But if they did, our only course would be nonviolent resistance. And how effective can that be? A very instructive survey has been made of cases in various lands in the book *Nonviolence* by William Robert Miller (New York, 1964). Here is a brief summary of his findings.

In Hungary such movements go back a century. The feud then was with Austria. Deak, the Hungarian leader, by "able statesmanship, patience, and passive resistance," achieved in 1867 the restoration of the Hungarian constitution. But he was aided by circumstance. Austria was being pressed by Germany and could not afford to be weakened through conflict with Hungary.

Today and What Next?

In 1956 Hungary's conflict was with Russia. When the demonstrations began, tanks were sent in. The demonstrators and the invaders at first fraternized until some Hungarian communist guards fired on the demonstrators. The Russians thought the fraternization had been a ruse and joined in giving fire. Russia then sent in 6000 tanks and 200,000 troops. The uprising was quelled, but the new regime instituted some of the reforms demanded and purged the Stalinists.

The East German rising in 1953 brought Russian intervention, but such was the sympathy of the Russian soldiers for the German workers that eighteen Soviet officers were executed for refusal to obey orders. Yet the uprising was suppressed.

The Finns demanded independence from Russia. The general strike of 1905 was successful, but only because Russia had been defeated by Japan.

In South Africa the results have been so disheartening that the pan-African conference in 1962 put the question, "Can a government bent on using the utmost force to crush the freedom struggle be forever countered by peaceful and nonviolent means?" The answer was an unequivocal "No!" Fifteen years later the prospect was unaltered.

In Ghana, Nkrumaj gained victory by bringing the economic life of the country to a standstill through a general strike, and, having won, introduced a fascist regime.

The Danish resistance to the Germans did not end the occupation, but under the very eyes of the German sea patrols the resisters were able to evacuate 7,500 Jews to other lands.

In Norway, the attempt of Quisling to nazify the schools and youth and to set up a corporate state was defeated.

In the United States, the civil rights movement was initiated by blacks who disobeyed local ordinances of segregation in school and on buses. Violent resistance by whites was not resisted. The blacks overcame.

Miller's conclusion is that "historic crises resolved solely by pure nonviolence are virtually nonexistent."

This verdict does not seem to me to fit the case of the American blacks. They have been vindicated by the Supreme Court and the civil rights legislation. The country was not intimidated into these steps by external force. The victory of the blacks was the response of the white conscience. One must at the same time recognize that sometimes goals are achieved only because of some extraneous circumstance as in the cases of Hungary and Finland.

All of this evidence as to the effectiveness of nonviolent resistance wears the air of asking how best to withstand the Russians were they to invade our country. But we are much more concerned to make sure that they do not. Universal disarmament alone will not deter them and for that matter it would be impossible without a thorough reordering of our economic life to absorb the dislocated as just noted, and of our political life to subordinate the national to the international. We need some form of world government.

The United Nations should be developed into a world state dealing with situations involving international relations. Local matters would be left to localities.[192] Friction within the world state between power blocks would be greatly reduced by the disbanding of national armies. The world government should operate in conjunction with a world court operating in accord with an accepted body of international law. A measure of coercion could not be avoided if some group flouted the rulings. One would hope that economic sanctions would suffice to bring compliance. A peace corps would be needed to deal with flashes of violence. It should be equipped with the best devices technology

can invent (technology is not to be scrapped) to subdue mobs
without loss of life.

This then is our goal and obviously it involves vastly more
than our own security. By what strategy is it to be pursued? If
strikes, lockouts, boycotts, sit-ins and parades are ineffective, is
there anything left? Persuasion. In any case this is where to
begin and keep on. The lead may be taken by a ruler who seeks
to mold the mind of his country. It may be the campaign of an
elite for sanity and humanity. It may be a demonstration of the
underprivileged, appealing both to idealism and self-interest. It
may be the alliance of a ruler and a prophet. This was suggested
in the previous section. Now for a striking example.[193]

The ruler was William Pitt, the prophet, William Wilberforce.
The cause was the abolition of the slave trade and then of slavery
itself in the British dominions. The two were the most intimate
of friends and often larked together. Pitt was prime minister,
Wilberforce a member of Parliament at an early age. Both de-
sired the abolition of slavery. Wilberforce, after an evangelical
experience of conversion, resolved to make this cause his sole
concern. Pitt knew that he could not give it priority in every
session and remain in office. He had also other objectives, one
of which was to keep Napoleon from dominating Europe.

After decades of agitation, Wilberforce addressed Parliament
in May of 1798 and presented a true picture of the condition of
the slaves in contrast to that drawn by a colleague:

> Mr. Morris, the delegate from Liverpool, tells the
> House that the apartments of the captives are fitted up as
> much for their advantage as circumstances will admit.
> They have several meals a day, some of their own coun-
> try provisions with the best sauces of African cookery.
> After breakfast they have water to wash themselves,

while their apartments are perfumed with frankincense and lime juice. Before dinner they are amused in the manner of their country. The song and dance are promoted. The men play and sing, while the women and girls make fanciful ornaments with beads with which they are plentifully supplied.

Wilberforce replied:

We have it on the concurrent testimony of other witnesses that the food is horse beans and water is scarce. As for frankincense and lime juice, the stench is intolerable. The song and dance are *promoted*. To make them exercise, though loaded with chains, they are forced to dance with the lash. As for singing, their songs of lamentations are so mournful that a captain threatened to flog the women if they did not stop. There is one piece of irrefutable evidence, death. The rate of mortality between capture and sale is 50 percent and the deaths of seamen in the slave trade far exceed those in the merchant vessels. We are told that if England gives up the trade France will continue. France is too enlightened a country for that. But even so, shall we rob and murder because if we do not someone else will? Let us put an end at once to this infamous traffic! Let us stop this effusion of human blood!

This speech was delivered when Wilberforce was forty years old. Victory was yet many years in coming. And then his prediction proved correct that others would continue the trade and supply the British dominions. The only answer was the total abolition of slavery itself in those parts. Wilberforce agitated unceasingly. He was on the point of death when in 1833 the

House voted not only to abolish slavery but to indemnify the owners. "Thank God," he exclaimed, "that I have lived to witness the day in which England is willing to give twenty million sterling for the abolition of slavery." Had he lived but one more year he would have received the news that on 31 July 1834, 800,000 slaves had become free.

This example is both heartening and disheartening. The goal was achieved but after what a time! Social change is slow: a century from emancipation to civil rights in the United States; four hundred years from the best saying on religious liberty to its realization in the West. On the other hand, we are heartened to note that sometimes wealth and power make voluntary renunciations. One is also cheered that, although at times the prophet and the ruler were at odds over policy, the personal bond was never ruptured and fittingly Wilberforce and Pitt lie side by side in Westminster Abbey.

Where then are we? Some are able to look with equanimity on the prospect of the speedy extinction of the human race. For them our relationship to God is all that matters. They are, of course, right that the human race cannot exist indefinitely on this planet. "When the sun grows cold, and the moon grows old, and the leaves of the judgment book unfold," [194] all the superb achievements of man will be "an unsubstantial pageant faded." [195] True, but one will not say that our relationship to God is all that matters if one has great-grandchildren who may have yet close to another century to live. And there are millions like them. Their future is our concern. If we are wise to understand our problems, if we are disciplined to tighten our belts, if we are courageous in meeting the challenges of the present and those to come, there may yet be millennia for people on earth. But better to be wiped out than to survive by sinking lower than beasts and barbarians.

The Historian's Craft

The reader who has ploughed through these pages would like to know how the historians know what they claim to know or is history just "a lie agreed upon"? The question is, of course, acute for the historians. The first question is how to find the evidence, the second to know whether it is reliable, and the third to assess what it is all about.

The prior question is to decide how much of the past is history. There is the history of the planet before it was able to sustain human life, and there is the history of living creatures before ever one worthy to be called man emerged. The first is the province of geology, the second of biology. History usually is taken to be that which relates the course of man. But here a distinction is made between the pre- and the post-historic. The distinction is invalid because they overlap. Archeology reveals for us not only the mode of life but also something of the ideas of primitive man which carry over. For the way of living we have axe heads, arrowheads, pottery, jewelry and the like. As for beliefs, the articles buried with the corpse witness to a belief in an afterlife. Then artifacts may bear inscriptions. There is, for example, the *Monumentum Ancyranum* which lists the achievements of the reign of Augustus.

Archeology may confirm, confute or augment the literary sources. J. B. Bury's *History of Greece* went through successive editions during the course of fifty years in order to take account of the new archeological findings. Archeology may vindicate the essential accuracy of written narratives. Schiedeman's excavation of Troy demonstrated that Homer was not simply writing fiction, and the unearthing of Mykini validated the historicity of Agamemnon. An inscription of Gallio confirms the statement in Acts 18 that he was the governor of Achaia.

Archeology sometimes disposes of an assumption. Constantine himself averred that he had been converted at the time of the battle of the Mulvian bridge in 311. The historian Grégoire asserted that the date must be wrong because each of the contestants in the struggle for empire sought to find favor in the area yet to be conquered by letting it be known that in case of victory the religion there prevailing would have governmental favor. But Constantine in 311 was fighting for control of the West where Christianity was not the dominant religion. Consequently his adherence to the faith must be postponed for ten years until he was struggling for control of the East where Christianity was in the ascendance. His theory is disproved by the discovery of a coin minted in 313 bearing on it the monogram of Christ. To allow time for the minting this would take us back certainly earlier than 313 and not far from the date of the battle of the Mulvian bridge. The point is of interest in showing that Constantine did not embrace the faith for the sake of a political advantage, except perhaps in the sense of hope that the Christian God would help him.

At the same time archeology often does not tell us what an artifact is all about. Without a literary source to provide an explanation we may be at a loss. In Japan I saw a traveling exhibition of ancient Bulgarian icons. One showed doubting Thomas pointing his finger at the wound of Christ. The caption was "St. Tom's treachery." Obviously the Japanese curator had not read the gospels. He might have consulted them, but sometimes there is nothing to consult. The architectural remains of Mithraism are abundant, the literary remains exceedingly scant. Since so many of the mithraia are found in the areas on the frontiers, where garrisons were stationed, we can infer that this religion was popular among soldiers. The cosmology has to be pieced together after scrupulous examination of the many remains.

The technique of deduction from vestiges, traces, tracks, and remains has been described by Renier.[196] As a model he cited the case of Robinson Crusoe as imagined by Defoe. Crusoe, believing himself to be on an absolutely uninhabited island, finds on the sand the imprint of a human foot. He is dumbfounded and proceeds to speculate as to how it could have occurred. Was it a dream? He went back to check and there it still was. Could it have been caused by Satan?—a surmise impossible in our day. And it did not satisfy him in his day. The conclusion was that it must have been made by a human foot. But was it his own foot? No, it didn't match.

But now his correct inference required some prior information. Augustine well observed that if one found the tracks of a cow in a meadow, one would not know that they had been made by a cow if one had never seen a cow. One could infer something. The tracks had been made by an animal with a cloven hoof and it must have been larger than a boar. Where we have a complete dinosaur skeleton the reconstruction can have a high degree of verisimilitude.

Still, inference may be taken to prove altogether too much. In the twelfth century there was an Albigensian who believed in the transmigration of souls.[197] He recalled that in his previous incarnation he had been a horse. Under the spur of his master he had leapt forward and caught a foot in a crevice between two rocks. The shoe pulled off. After he became a man he went back to that very spot and there was the horseshoe. Now this proves the doctrine of transmigration, or does it?

Thus far we have been considering archeological artifacts. The problem is in a way even more difficult in the case of written documents. The artifacts are originals. The written documents for antiquity are almost invariably copies. If there is only one copy, as in the case of Trajan's letter to Pliny about the Christians, there can be no dispute over variant readings and no certainty that the one copy is correct. But when, as in the case of the New Testament, we have hundreds of manuscripts, textual criticism becomes a highly specialized discipline. There are many variant readings and by what criteria do we determine authenticity? There are some rules. The shorter reading is to be preferred because a scribe copying the very word of God, might amplify but would never deliberately omit. I noticed the tendency to expand in a translation of the New Testament into modern Greek. The translator faithfully renders, "There was no room for them in the inn," and then adds, "You see, Bethlehem was crowded by all those who had come to register for the census."

Another rule is that the harder reading is to be preferred, that is the reading which is the most difficult to understand. The scribe would simplify it, unless, of course, he were an existentialist philosopher. A further check results from the grouping of texts. We have, for example, the Western and the Eastern texts. The latter in most cases is superior and if there is no other test, its reading is preferred.

Sometimes a translation shows which text was utilized by a translator. This possibility occasioned a long-lived error in the case of the Trinitarian verse in 1 John 3:5. "There are three in heaven that witness, the Father, the Spirit, and the Son." Erasmus omitted this verse in the earliest printed edition of the Greek Testament in 1516. There was a shriek of outrage with the charge that he was denying the doctrine of the Trinity. He retorted that he was doing nothing of the sort. The point was simply that the verse was not in the manuscripts at his disposal. If one were found in Greek he would restore it in his next edition. None had been found by 1519 and it was still lacking in the edition of that year. But then someone did come up with a copy containing the verse. Erasmus suspected a forgery, and we know that he was right. But he kept his word and inserted it into the edition of 1522, justifying himself on the ground that it was in the Latin translation of St. Jerome in the fourth century. Surely Jerome would never have made it up. He must have found it in the Greek manuscript before him. What Erasmus did not know was that the verse did not get into the manuscripts of Jerome's translation until the eighth century. A translation cannot be used to check an original unless we have the original of the translation. The consequence of the error lasted until our own day. Luther used the edition in 1519 where it did not appear and consequently remained out of the German renderings. But Tyndale used the edition of 1522 and it went into all of the English versions until removed in the Revised Standard Version of our own day.

When the text of the documents has been established as accurately as possible, then comes the task of interpreting behavior and ideas. If the contemporary accounts differ in their appraisal of men and movements, which are we to choose? Can we divine the motives of the actors? If they declared their motives, were they sincere or seeking to beguile? Were they not even conscious of their real motives? Here it is that the psychiatrists enter in the attempt by way of hints to uncover underlying drives. The attempt is worth making but the method highly precarious. The dead cannot be put on the couch. Furthermore, the psychiatrist is apt to impose a preconceived estimate of human nature on the departed. Once I sat in a train in front of a middle-aged man who was conversing with a young lady. After she left, he and I struck up a conversation. He said to me, "You can't imagine what a relief it was to talk with that girl. She is training to be a teacher of Hebrew. She knows where she is going. I spend my days listening to young people who don't know where they are going." His clinical experience with the unbalanced might well make it difficult for him to understand the balanced, though in this instance clearly he did.

Freud, in writing biography, was on the lookout for the Oedipus complex and homosexuality. As to the first, by the way, he completely distorted the Oedipus legend. For Freud it meant the craving of a male to sleep with his mother and kill his father. In the legend, Oedipus married his mother without knowing that she was his mother, and killed his father without knowing that he was his father. As for homosexuality, Freud finds it in Leonardo da Vinci on no better evidence than that he had no ladyfriend and used boys for models.

Adler and Erikson believe that the great human impulse is the drive for power. With this presupposition, Erikson assumes that Luther became a monk to free himself from his father and be somebody in his own right.[198] Later he broke with the church in order to found one of his own. Luther said that he went into the monastery because he was commanded by God in a thunderstorm. The comment to that may be, "That's what he said but underneath he was trying to extricate himself from a clash with his father by becoming a monk." There is no evidence, however, that he was having a clash with his father. The other instance is completely unambiguous. He did not leave the church to found one of his own. He did not leave. He was expelled. And he did not seek to found a church of his own. He had been secreted in the castle of the Wartburg under peril of his life when a plea came from the town council at Wittenberg that he come back to calm the turbulence of his followers. At great risk he returned and a church emerged.

How far can the historian be projected into the past? Never completely, but one can steep oneself for a decade in the literature of a period until one has knowledge and feeling for the circumstances, presupposition, moral codes, and religious ideas of the age. The historian may start with a hypothesis, not in order to prove it, but to test it. The past cannot be reenacted but in a sense it must be relived. To understand one must have experienced something comparable. The historian Bloch said that he would never have understood the feelings of a defeated country had he not been in Paris when the Germans marched in.[199] To comprehend tragedy one must at some point have been struck in the midriff.

Should the historian be confined to a single discipline? Febvre pled for the interdisciplinary.[200] He was absolutely right, though one must not overlook the varieties of method in different disciplines. The history of science is a branch of inspirational literature. Who now goes to Galen, Hippocrates, Ptolemy, Copernicus, Harvey, and Newton for science? What they have done they have done. One reads their biographies for inspiration to emulate their examples. The history of ideas is not so time-bound. We do read Plato for philosophy and Paul or Aquinas for theology, not to mention the long line of their successors.

But despite disparities there is interplay. Christian ideas have profoundly affected every discipline in the history of the western world. In art one thinks at once of Dürer, Michelangelo, and

Rembrandt, in music of Bach, Handel and Beethoven, and so on. The natural sciences have demolished biblical cosmology. But theology has played a part in scientific discovery. Take the case of Michael Servetus, the discoverer of the pulmonary circulation of the blood. He was prompted to engage with Vesalius in dissection by the statement in Genesis that the soul is in the blood. How then is the soul able to make itself felt in every part of the body? Only because the blood travels. Does physiology bear out the assumption? He discovered that the bloodstream does not seep through the wall of the heart but by way of the pulmonary artery passes to the lungs, there changes color, returns to the other side of the heart and then is dispersed throughout the body. Theologically he needed the full circulation. Lacking a microscope to disclose the capillaries, he could not go further physiologically than the pulmonary circulation. Another point was the connection of inspiration and respiration. The Lord God *breathed* life into Adam. The blood then is aerated in the lungs and respiration is thus related to inspiration. Obviously we cannot reason in the same fashion as Servetus but we can observe the interrelation of disciplines.

Another proposal of Febvre is that historians should work in teams. For the collection of data that is certainly possible. There are in this country a number of groups centering on one phase of the Reformation or another, the field with which I am most familiar. Half a dozen are working in the Reformation in Spain, several in France, others in Italy and England. Some have chosen cities such as Nürnberg and Strasbourg. The radical Reformation, comprising enthusiasts, rationalists, sectarians and the like are receiving no little collaborative attention. These groups are not schools in the sense of working in a single locality. They come to know each other through published articles and professional gatherings, which often are chiefly valuable by way of personal acquaintance. I remember a Luther congress at Aarhus in Denmark in 1957. When we had all been introduced, Gordon Rupp said, "We've met each other. Let's go home." I wonder often about the papers. Frequently they are of the sort which should be published in professional journals to be read leisurely and pondered.

Febvre encouraged also the full use of technology. There is really no need to stress that any more. Xerox has become as universal as it is now well nigh indispensable. How I remember that in 1926 I lugged a heavy Hammond typewriter on my back around Europe copying whole books in Latin. Of course, we had photostats then but I could not afford them. And now we have the computer. It is superb for a concordance. I am told that the one for the Revised Standard Version of the Bible was done in weeks rather than in years by hand. The computer facilitates the organization of data. The danger now is that scholars will be so enthused about this new gadget that they will start computerizing what isn't worth knowing.

Finally there is style, and that's hard to define. Certainly we should avoid the verbose, ponderous, reverberating like the chords of an organ in an empty cathedral, and the parenthetical, which expands a sentence to a page. The style must be individual so that one who knows the author can say, "Sounds just like him or her," provided, of course, that the sound is not insufferable. As for varieties, I received a lesson by reading the work of my great uncle, George Bainton, entitled *The Art of Authorship*. He solicited and compiled from the distinguished Victorians statements on their methods in writing. From the variety I concluded that one could do no better than choose one's own method and stick to it. And the same may be said of style.

As for specialization for colleagues versus simplification for the public, there is a dual responsibility. The acquisition of knowledge and the advance in insight are not merely to be passed around among ourselves. There is an obligation to disseminate.

And now a further word on the measure in which the historian must be of the past in order to understand the past. To be of the past does not require that one be an antique. Past and present are indissoluable. Human experience, despite the many varieties, has a fundamental unity. One does not need to be hundreds of years old to understand an inscription on an ancient tombstone by a husband in memory of his wife. "The Lord has chastened me for my shortcomings. She has been taken. I am alone." Of this I am convinced that one can never understand the religion of the past who has not been brushed by the winged seraph, nor said with St. Augustine, "My soul is restless until it find its rest in Thee."

Notes

1. *Historismus* has borne various senses for which the article by Dwight E. Lee and Robert N. Beck, "The Meaning of 'Historicism,'" *Am. Hist. Rev.* LIX, 3 (1953-1954), pp. 368-377. The core idea seems to me to be individualism in the treatment by Friedrich Meinecke, *Die Entstehung des Historismus, Werke* III (1958-1969). Wilhelm Dilthey expressed his view in "Beiträge zum Studien der Individualität," *Sitzungsberichte der König. Ak. der Wiss.* XIII (1i96), pp. 1-41. Ernst Troeltsch's initial view is in *Der Historismus und seine Uberwindung* (reprinted 1966). His later article entitled "On Natural Law and Humanity" is in English in Otto Gierke, *Natural Law and the Theory of Society 1500-1800* (Cambridge, 1958).
2. Jaspers, Karl, *Origin and Goal of History* (London, 1953), pp. 244ff.
3. Bainton, Roland H., *El Alma Hispania y el Alma Sajona* (La Aurora, Buenos Aires, Argentina, 1961).
4. Bainton, Roland H., *Hunted Heretic, The Life and Death of Michael Servetus* (Boston, 1953).
5. Toynbee, Arnold, *Experiences* (Oxford, 1969), p. 35.
6. Pliny, *Nat. Hist.* X Biii.
7. "The Respite of Nero," poem by C. P. Cavary in *Four Greek Poets,* ed. Kelly and Sherrard (Penguin, reprint 1970), p. 21.
8. Herodotus, *Hist.* Bk. I, sec. 53. The preceding section tells of Croesus' futile attempt to thwart the prediction of the death of his son.

Notes

9. Patch, Howard Rollin, "The Tradition of the Goddess Fortuna," *Smith College Studies in Modern Languages* VIII, 3, April 1922.
10. *Il Principe* XXV, *Opere* (1969), pp. 63-64.
11. Spengler, Oswald, *Untergang des Abendlandes* II, 208.
12. Bainton, Roland H., *Here I Stand* (Nashville, 1950), pp. 101, 186-187.
13. Bainton, Roland H., "Probleme der Lutherbiographie," *Luther-Forschung Heute* (Berlin, 1958), pp. 24ff.
14. Toynbee, *Experiences,* p. 36.
15. Muller, Robert J., *Uses of the Past* (New York, Oxford, 1952), p. 35.
16. *Meditations* XI.
17. Polybius, *Historia* VI (Loeb Library, pp. 438-9). Further examples are given by Walther Rehm, *Der Untergang Roms in abendländischen Denken* (Leipzig, 1920), pp. 11ff. Pindar, *Nem. Od.* VI has merely a deterministic theory. Plato in *Rep.* VIII, III observes recurrent dissolution and renewal; so also Lucretius, *De Rerum Natura* V, 813-23 and Cicero *Rep.* II, 25.
18. Vico, Giambattista, in *La Scienza Nuova,* I (Bari, 1928).
19. *Catalina,* ch. I-X, fragments 11-12.
20. *Ep.* VII.
21. Fenne, Thomas, *Fennes Frutes* (1590), fol. 53.
22. Bury, J. B., *The Idea of Progress* (New York, 1955).
23. Hegel, Georg W., *Philosophy of History* (World's Great Classics, New York, 1899).
24. Tuveson, Ernest Lee, *Millenium and Utopia* (Berkeley, 1949).
25. Documentation for the above paragraph in R. H. Bainton, *Christian Attitudes to War and Peace* (Nashville, 1960), pp. 20-22 and notes.
26. Matthew 13:39.
27. Müntzer, Thomas, *Fürstenpredigt,* 1524. Cf. Otto G. Brandt, *Thomas Müntzer, Sein Leben und Schriften* (1953), p. 162.
28. Marshall, Stephen, *Song of Moses* (London, 1643).
29. Sorel, George, *Illusions of Progress* (Berkeley, 1961).
30. For the sources on Phalaris see Roland H. Bainton, *Castellio Concerning Heretics* (New York, 1935), p. 134, note 29.
31. Aeschylus, *Seven Against Thebes,* tr. Gilbert Murray (London). Lines 345-351.
32. Thucydides V, 85-96.
33. Tacitus, *Agricola* 30.
34. Orosius, *Seven Books* VI, 1.
35. Justinus, *Epit. Pompei Trogi* XXVIII, 2.

Notes

36. Horace, *Epode* VII.
37. Delitzsch, Friedrich "Asurbanipal," *Der alte Orient* XI (1909).
38. Seneca, *Naturales Quaestiones* III Praef.
39. Quintius Curtius, *Res Gestae Alexandri* VII, 8, 15.
40. Tarn, William Woodthorpe, *Alexander the Great* II (Cambridge, England, 1948) commenting on Diodorus Siculus 46, 4 and chap. XVII.
41. This Arria was the wife of Caecina Paetus. The source is Mart. 1, 14 and Pliny, *Ep.* 111, 16. Arria, the wife of Paetus Thrasea, was minded to do the like but restrained by her husband's plea that she save herself for their child. Tacitus XVI, section 34.
42. Marcus Attilius Regulus referred to in Cicero *In Pisonem* XIX. And Augustine *De Civitate Die* 1, 14 and 24.
43. Tacitus, *Historia* III, 25, 81.
44. Mr. Luce was one of the visitors. I have condensed the account.
45. From Norman Lewis, *Sunday Times Colour Magazine*, Feb. 23, 1968. Reprinted in *Win*, March 31, 1977.
46. Auerbach, Erich, *Mimesis* (New York, 1957), pp. 36-38.
47. Letter to Arsacius in B. J. Kidd, *Documents Illustrative of the History of the Church* II, no. 34 (London, 1923).
48. Jordan, Wilbur Kitchener, *Philanthropy in England 1480-1660* (London, 1959).
49. Gal. 2:20.
50. Packard, Vance, *The People Shapers* (Boston, 1977).
51. Castellio, Sebastian, *Conseil à la France Désolée* (1562, reprint 1967), p. 46.
52. Caesar of Heisterbach, cited in G. G. Coulton, *Five Centuries* II (1927), p. 17.
53. Norwood, Frederick, *Strangers and Exiles* (Nashville, Tenn., 1969).
54. *Daedalus* 1976 (the entire issue on Gibbon).
55. Jones, W. H. S., *A Neglected Factor in the History of Greece and Rome* (Cambridge, 1907); *Malaria and Greek History* (Manchester, 1909); *Disease and History* (Hastings, 1909).
56. Zinsser, Hans, *Rats, Lice and History* (Boston, 1935). McNeill, William Hardy, *Plagues and People* (1976).
57. MacMullen (listed above), pp. 335-337.
58. Huntington, Ellsworth, *Civilization and Climate* (New Haven, 1915). "Climactic Change and Agricultural Exhaustion," *Q. Jr. Econ.* XXXI, No. 2, Feb. 1917. On the decline of agriculture in Italy, Vladimir Simkovitch, *Pol Sci. Q.*, XXXI (1916), pp. 201-243.

Notes

59. P. Petit, *Précis d'Histoire Ancienne* (Paris, 1965²), p. 344.

60. Ammianus Marcellinus, XXIII, 6, 64.

61. Jones, A. H. M., *The Decline of the Ancient World* (New York, 1961), p. 362.

62. Montesquieu thought the extension too rapid (see Rehm, p. 100). Wallbank suggests that Trajan extended the empire too widely, p. 36.

63. See my *Erasmus of Christendom* (New York, 1969), p. 118.

64. Salmon, E. T. *The Nemesis of Empire* (London, 1974). Rostovtzeff, *History of the Ancient World, II Rome* (Oxford, 1926) makes a similar point that the aristocracy, having achieved power, did not keep it through failure to imbue the populace with its ideals.

65. Tacitus, *Annals* XV, xliv.

66. Barrow, Reginald H., *Slavery in the Roman Empire* (London, 1928). Rollins, Wayne G., "Slavery in the New Testament," in *The Interpreter's Dictionary of the Bible* (Nashville, 1976), provides an excellent article and up-to-date bibliography on slavery in the empire.

67. *Ep.* 47.

68. Haywood, Richard M., *The Myth of Rome's Fall* (New York, 1958).

69. MacMullen, Ramsay, "Barbarian Enclaves in the Northern Roman Empire," *L'Antiquité Classique* 32 (1963), pp. 353-361.

70. On anti-Gothic feeling Haywood, listed above. For Synesius, *Letters and Address to Arcadius,* tr. Aug. Fitzgerald (Oxford, 1926). Cf. Georg Grützmacher, *Synesios v. Kyrene* (Leipzig, 1913). On the military situation Robert Grosse, *Römische Militargeschichte* (Berlin, 1920), 260-265.

71. *De Civ. Dei* I, 1-3.

72. *Seven Books,* VI, 1.

73. *On the Government of God,* tr. Sanford (New York, 1930) VII, 20, p. 216.

74. Luke 12:20.

75. John 12:24.

76. Compare my *Erasmus of Christendom* (New York, 1969), p. 189.

77. *Institutio, Corpus Reformatorum* IX, 289-90.

78. Jung, C. C., *Answer to Job* (London, 1958).

79. Matt. 5:45, condensed.

80. Luke 13:1-5.

81. John 9:1-3.

Notes

82. Lucretius, *De Rerum Natura* VI, 387f. and 639.
83. Augustine, *Confessions* VIII, iii.
84. Judg. 11:30ff.
85. Kenworthy, Leonard, *World View* (Richmond, Ind., 1977).
86. The condensation of Luther's version is from my *Here I Stand* (Nashville, 1950), pp. 368-370. See my account of the interchange in *Erasmus of Christendom* and *Here I Stand*.
87. Schweitzer, Albert, *Quest of the Historic Jesus* (London, 1911).
88. Paulus, Heinrich E. G., *Das Leben Jesu,* 4 vols. (Leipzig, 1828), 1, 35.
89. Schleiermacher summarized in David Friedrich Strauss, *Das Leben Jesu* (Leipzig, 1864), pp. 22f.
90. Strauss, *op. cit.*
91. John 6:9 and 13; Moses in Numbers 11:21f., Elisha, 2 Kings 4:43.
92. Bacon, Benjamin W., *Beginnings of Gospel Story* (New Haven, 1909), p. 78, on Mark 6:35f. and 8:1ff.
93. Mark 8:20 and Acts 6:3.
94. Kalthoff, Albert, *Das Christus-Problem* (Leipzig, 1903[2]), p. 89.
95. Kautsky, Karl, Foundations of Christianity (London, 1925).
96. Matt. 10:34.
97. Drews, Arthur, *The Christ Myth* (Chicago, 1911).
98. Deissmann, Gustav Adolf, *Licht von Osten* (Tübingen, 1923).
99. Details in Paul Schmiedel, article Gospels in *Enc. Biblica* II. Further examples in Wilhelm Heitmüller, *Jesus* (Tübingen, 1913).
100. Mark 10:17; Matt. 19:6.
101. Luke 11:29-30; Matt. 12:39-40.
102. Mark 14:36; Matt. 26:30; Luke 22:42; John 12:27.
103. Heb. 4:15; 2 Cor. 5:21.
104. John chapter 1.
105. Matt. 11:11.
106. Acts 18:26.
107. Mark 3:21 and 31-35.
108. *American Journal of Theology* for 1911, a number of articles on this theme. McFadden, Thomas, ed., *Does Jesus Make a Difference?* (1974).
109. Harrisville, Roy A., *Frank Chamberlain Porter* (Missoula, Mont., 1976), p. 66.
110. Tillich, Paul, *The Interpretation of History* (New York, 1936), pp. 33, 59, 250-265.
111. John 14:9.

Notes

112. Brandon, S. G. F., *Jesus and the Zealots* (Manchester, 1967).
113. Luke 1:32; Mark 10:35; Luke 24:21; Acts 1:6.
114. Bultmann, Rudolf, works in English translation:
    Essays Philosophical and Theological (London, 1955).
    Existence and Faith (New York, 1960).
    Faith and Understanding (New York, 1969).
    Jesus Christ and Mythology (New York, 1958).
    Symposia dealing with his ideas:
      Anderson, Hugh, ed. *Jesus* (Englewood Cliffs, NJ, 1969).
      Bartsch, Hans W., ed., *Kerygma and Myth* (London, 1957).
      Braaten, Carl E., and Roy Harrisville, ed., *Kerygma and History* (New York, 1962).
      Kegley, Charles W., ed., *The Theology of Rudolf Bultmann* (New York, 1966).
    Individual Evaluations:
      Künneth, Walter, *Glauben an Jesus?* (Hamburg, 1962).
      Owen, H. P., *Revelation and Existence* (Cardiff, 1957).
      Robinson, Roger, *The Origins of Demythologizing* (Leiden, 1974).
115. Acts 9:36-39.
116. 2 Kings 17:17-24.
117. Matt. 12:17.
118. *Philostrati De Vita* IV, xvi.
119. Mark 5:29, Luke 8:41.
120. Luke 24:36, Matt. 28:17.
121. John 20:27.
122. Vermes, Geza, *Jesus the Jew* (London, 1973).
123. John 20:13.
124. Luke 24:34.
125. 1 Cor. 15:6.
126. Mark 16.
127. Matt. 28.
128. Luke 24.
129. John 20–21.
130. Luke 24:23.
131. John 20:26.
132. 1 Cor. 15:8.
133. Gal. 1:15-16.
134. Rom. 6:1-4.
135. PNF 14, 52 and 65.
136. *It Is My Belief* (London, 1953), for both of the above.

Notes

137. Steffens, Lincoln, *Autobiography* (New York, 1931), pp. 525-526.

138. 1 Cor. 15:9-12.

139. Knox, John, *Humanity and Divinity of Christ* (Cambridge, Eng., 1967).

140. Biblical references in the above paragraph: Rom. 8:2; Phil. 2:7; Gal. 4:4; 1 John 4:8.

141. Biblical references: Phil. 2:6-7; 2 Cor. 6:9; Heb. 2:17; Mark 13:32 and 9:1; Matt. 16:28.

142. Biblical references: Col. 1:15-19; John 1:1-8, 3:16; Rom. 4:25 and 5:11.

143. Dante, *De Monarchia*.

144. Biblical references: John 12:27; Luke 22:42; Matt. 26:39; Mark 14:36.

145. Schoonenberg, Piet, "Emptied Himself," *Concilium* II (New York, 1965), pp. 47-66.

146. Biblical references: Acts 2:36; Rom. 1:3; Heb. 5:10.

147. Biblical references: Mark 1:11; Heb. 2:9; Phil. 2:8-9; Rom. 1:3.

148. Biblical references: Heb. 5:8 and 2:8-9; Rom. 1:3.

149. Fuller, Reginald H., *The Foundations of New Testament Christology* (New York, 1965).

150. Biblical references: 2 Cor. 5:21; Heb. 4:14.

151. Luke 2:48.

152. *Tischreden* 7075.

153. Huxley, Thomas Henry, "The Keepers of the Herd of Swine," *Essays upon some Controversial Questions* (New York, 1892).

154. An observation of my esteemed cousin Harold J. Blackham, *The Human Tradition* (London, 1953), p. 114.

155. Bornkamm, Günther, *Jesus of Nazareth* (New York, 1969), p. 40.

156. The differences within Pharisaism are brought out by the Jewish scholar Asher Finkel, *The Pharisees and the Teacher of Nazareth,* (Brill, Leiden, 1964). Another Jewish scholar John Bauker, *Jesus and the Pharisees* (Cambridge, Eng., 1973) gives in English translation all of the available material on the Pharisees in the time of Jesus.

157. Biblical references: Luke 7:36; 11:37; 13:31; 14:1; and John 19:39.

158. Matt. 3:15.

159. Heb. 12:2.

160. Vermes, Geza, *Jesus the Jew* (London, 1973).

Notes

161. Biblical references: Luke 22:48; 9:58; 9:26; 16:28. Cf. Nils Dahl, *The Crucified Messiah* (Minneapolis, 1974).
162. Dodd, C. H., *The Founder of Christianity* (New York, 1970), p. 93.
163. Mark 10:45.
164. Matt. 11:27.
165. Vermes, *op. cit.*
166. Biblical references: Matt. 13:57; Mark 6:4; Luke 4:24; 13:33; John 4:19; Luke 7:30; Matt. 21:11.
167. Vermes, *op. cit.*, p. 224.
168. Tillich, Paul, *Systematic Theology* I (1954), p. 157.
169. Stowe, Harriet Beecher, "The Minister's Wooing," *Writings* V, pp. 253-254.
170. Dentan, Robert C., *The Idea of History in the Ancient Near East* (New Haven, Conn., 1955).
    Contains Millar Burrows, "Ancient Israel."
        Eric Dinkler, "Earliest Christianity."
        Roland Bainton, "Patristic Christianity."
171. Minear, Paul, *Images of the Church in the New Testament* (Philadelphia, 1960).
172. Matthew on prophecy: Virgin birth 1:23 a mistranslation of Is. 7:14; Bethlehem 2:16 cf. Micah 5:2; Egypt 2:15, cf. Hos. 11:1.
173. Biblical references: John 3:14; 1 Cor. 10:2; Heb. 11:17; Jas. 2:21.
174. 2 Peter 3:8-9.
175. Rev. 18:4.
176. Documentation in my *Christian Attitudes to War and Peace* (Nashville, Tenn., 1960). There is an excellent discussion in L. G. Patterson, *God and History in Early Christian Thought* (London, 1967). It is concerned with *thought*. I am interested even more in practice.
177. Biblical references: 2 Thess. 2; Rom. 2:14; Rom. 13.
178. Workman, H. B., *Persecution in the Early Church* (London, 1906).
179. See note 176 for coverage through Augustine.
180. On Augustine: Eric Dinkler, "Augustins Geschichtauffassung," *Schweitzerische Monatshefte* XXXIV (1954), 514-526.
    Mommsen, Theodore, "Saint Augustine and the Christian Idea of Progress," *Journal of the History of Ideas* XII, 3 (June, 1951), 346-374.
181. Niebuhr, H. Richard, *Christianity and Culture* (New York,

Notes

1951) finds more than three, but I am addicted to trinitarian groupings.

182. Coulton, G. G., *Five Centuries of Religion II* (Cambridge, Eng., 1955), p. 17.

183. Trueblood, Elton, "Vocational Christian Pacifism," *Christianity and Crisis* (Nov. 3, 1941).

184. Niebuhr was developing an observation of Ernst Troeltsch in *Der Historismus und seine Überwindung* (1966, 5th ed.), pp. 20-21.

185. Tacitus, *Annals* XV, 44.

186. Erasmus *EE* IV, 1239.

187. Waltz, Kenneth, *Man, the State and War* (New York, 1954).

188. Wheeler, John Harvey, "Democracy in a Revolutionary Era," *Center Occasional Paper* III, no. 3, 1970, p. 169.

189. Bainton, Roland H., *Christian Attitudes to War and Peace* (Nashville, 1960). The following pages summarize this book.

190. Ramsey, Paul, *War and the Christian Conscience* (New York, 1961), 181.

191. Melman, Seymour, ed., *Disarmament, Its Politics and Economics* (Boston, 1962).

192. Wheeler (note 188 above), p. 63 notes that "today's new nations could not have come into being without the United Nations."

193. Copeland, H., *Wilberforce* (Oxford, 1923).

194. Taylor, Bayard, *Bedouin Song.*

195. Shakespeare, *Tempest* IV, 8.

196. Renier, C. J., *History, Its Purpose and Method* (Boston, 1950).

197. Vacandard, Elphège, *The Inquisition* (New York, 1915), p. 60.

198. Erikson, Erik, *Young Man Luther* (New York, 1958).

199. Bloch, Marc, *The Historian's Craft* (New York, 1953).

200. Febvre, Lucien, *A New Kind of History,* ed. Peter Burck (New York, 1973).

Selected Bibliography

PHILOSOPHY OF HISTORY

Arnett, Willard E., *Modern Reader in the Philosophy of History* (New York, 1966).

Burckhardt, Jakob, *Weltgeschichtliche Betrachtungen* (Berlin, 1905).

Bury, J. B., *The Idea of Progress* (New York, 1955).

Butterfield, Herbert, *Man on His Past* (Boston, 1966).

Collingwood, R. G., *Essays in the Philosophy of History* (Univ. Texas, 1965).

Dilthey, Wilhelm, *Pattern and Meaning in History* (New York, 1961) and William Klubach, *Wilhelm Dilthey's Philosophy of History* (New York, 1956).

Gardiner, Patrick T., ed., *Theories of History* (New York, 1964).

Halperin, William, ed. *Essays in Modern European History* (Chicago, 1970).

Hegel, Georg W., "Philosophy of History," in *World Classics* (New York, 1899).

Heilbronner, Robert L., *The Future as History* (New York, 1959).

Herder, Johann von, *Reflections on the Philosophy of the History of Mankind* (Chicago, 1968).

Hexter, Jack H., *Reappraisals in History* (Evanston, 1967).

Holborn, Hajo, *History and the Humanities* (Garden City, New York, 1972).

Hook, Sidney, ed. *Philosophy and History* (New York, 1963).

Jaspers, Karl, *Origin and Goal of History* (London, 1953).

Kahler, Erich, *The Meaning of History* (New York, 1964).

Lewis, Bernard, *History Remembered, Recovered, Invented* (Princeton, 1975).

Bibliography

Löwith, Karl, *Meaning in History* (Chicago, 1949), extensive bibliography.

McIntire, C. T., editor, *God, History, and Historians, An Anthology of Modern Christian Views of History* (New York, 1977). The selections illustrate the reaction of Christian thinkers to the debacle of the idea of progress occasioned by the two world wars. Some of the writers sampled are historians, some literary figures, the majority are philosophers and theologians. There is an excellent bibliography.

Meyerhoff, Hans, ed. *The Philosophy of History in Our Time* (Garden City, NY, 1959).

Nash, Ronald H., *Ideas of History* (New York, 1963).

Niebuhr, Reinhold, *Faith and History* (New York, 1951).

Nietzsche, Friedrich, *The Use and Abuse of History* (New York, 1957).

Ott, Heinrich, "Neuere Publicationen zum Problem vom Geschichte und Geschicklichkeit," *Theologische Rundschau* XXI (1953), pp. 63-96.

Plumb, J. H., *The Death of the Past* (Boston, 1971).

Rickman, H. P., *Meaning in History* (On Dilthey), (London, 1961).

Sorel, George, *Illusion of Progress* (Berkeley, 1969).

Spengler, Oswald, *Decline of the West,* abridged (New York, 1965).

Tillich, Paul, *Interpretation of History* (New York, 1936).

Toynbee, Arnold, *Study of History,* abridged D. C. Somervell, 2 vols. (London, New York, 1946-1957).

Tuveson, Ernest Lee, *Millenium and Utopia* (Berkeley, 1949).

Widgery, Allen Gregory, *Interpretation of History,* excerpts (Berkeley, 1949).

———— *The Meaning in History* (London, 1967).

THE FALL OF ROME

Bury, J. B., "Causes of the Survival of the Roman Empire in the East" in *Selected Essays* (Chicago, 1967), pp. 231-242.

Chambers, Mortimer, ed., excerpts, *The Fall of Rome: Can It Be Explained?* (New York, 1963).

Haywood, Richard M., *The Myth of Rome's Fall* (New York, 1958).

Jones, A. H. M., *The Decline of the Ancient World* (New York, 1968).

MacMullen, Ramsay, *The Roman Government's Response to Crisis* (New Haven, 1976).

Muller, Herbert J., *Uses of the Past* (New York, 1952).

Perowne, Stewart, *The End of the Roman World* (New York, 1966).

Bibliography

Rehm, Walther, "Der Untergang Roms im abendländischen Denken," *Die Erbe des Alten,* 2 Reihe, Heft XVIII (Leipzig, 1930).

Salmon, E. T., *The Nemesis of Empire* (London, 1974).

Wallbank, F. N., *The Awful Revolution* (Toronto, 1969).

Werner, Heinrich, *Der Untergang Roms* (1939).

White, Lynn, ed., *The Transformation of the Roman World* (Berkeley, 1916).

CHRISTIANITY AND HISTORY

Butterfield, Herbert, *Christianity and History* (New York, 1950).

Cochrane, Charles Norris, *Christianity and Classical Culture* (Oxford, 1940).

Dawson, Christopher, selections ed. James Oliver and Christina Scott in *Religion and World History* (Garden City, New York, 1975).

Eddy, George Sherwood, *God in History* (New York, 1947).

Gilkey, Langdon, *Reaping the Whirlwind* (New York, 1976).

Harbison, E. Harris, *Christianity and History* (Princeton, 1964).

Harvey, Van Austin, *The Historian and the Believer* (New York, 1969). An admirable survey of the wrestlings of contemporary theologians with the question of how the faith of a historical religion fares if its origin in history is called into doubt.

Pannenberg, Wolfhart, "Weltgeschichte und Heilsgeschichte," in *Geschichte-Ereignis und Erzähling,* ed. Kostellek und Stempel (1973).

THE HISTORICAL JESUS

Bultmann, Rudolf. See note 114.

Fülling, Erich, "Geschichtlichkeit und Christentum in der Theologie der Gegenwart," *Studien der Lutherakademie,* N.F. 6.

Robinson, James McConkey, "A New Quest of the Historical Jesus," *Studies in Biblical Theology,* No. 25 (Naperville, Ill., 1925).

Schweitzer, Albert, *The Quest of the Historical Jesus* (London, 1910, New York, 1968).

THE RESURRECTION

Campenhausen, Hans Freiherr von, "Der Ablauf der Ostereignisse und das Leere Grab," *Sitzungsberichte der Heidelberg Ak. Phil. Hist. Kl.* 37-38, 1952-1954.

Niebuhr, R. R., *Resurrection and Historical Reason* (New York, 1957).

Perry, Michael, *The Easter Enigma* (Ld., 1959).

McLeman, James, *Resurrection Then and Now* (New York, 1967).